JOIE

CLARKSON POTTER/PUBLISHERS

NEW YORK

AJIRI AKI

PHOTOGRAPHS BY JESSICA ANTOLA

JOIE

A Parisian's Guide to Celebrating the Good Life

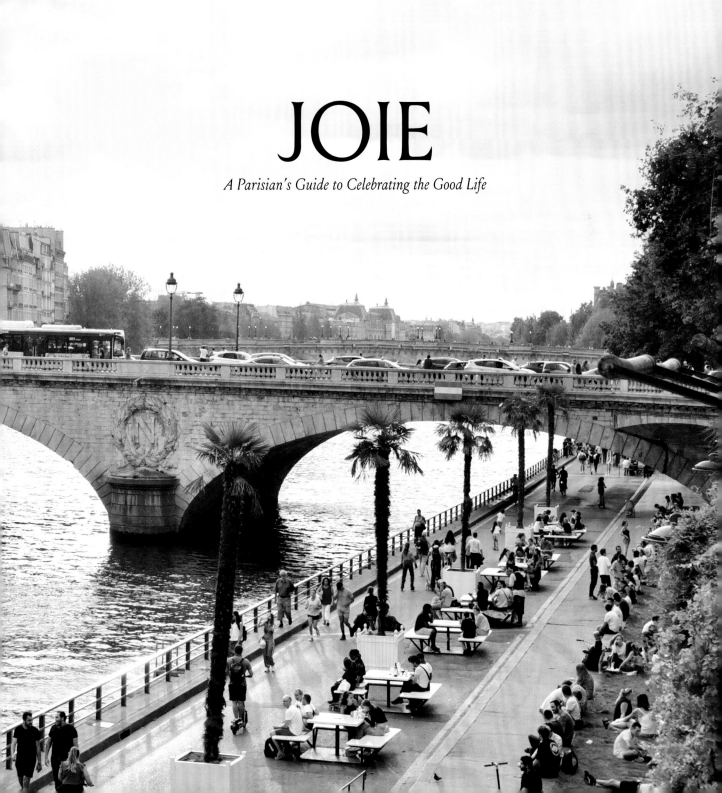

*To my mother, Cynthia, who introduced
me to the joy of fellowship, and to Thomas, who brought
me back to the city where I found my joie de vivre*

CONTENTS

INTRODUCTION

There's life, and then there's the good life.

I first traveled to Paris from New York for a single day as an undergrad and then again for a few months as a graduate student of the decorative arts. Those initial introductions opened my eyes to how Parisians lived so differently from me. But it was not until I returned for love, moving here permanently with my Swiss husband, and eventually became a mom to two very Parisian kids, that I took a closer look at the culture. I noticed the driving force behind the way the French live their lives.

It's joie de vivre. The joy of living.

Parisians find joy in what they eat, where they go, conversations they have, and how they spend their time. Simple things. It's their North Star. So, what does that look like? Instead of pushing a

shopping cart through a giant superstore to stock up on items in bulk, they might prefer to wait in a longer line for a single freshly made baguette from the local *boulangerie*. A stroll through the open-air *marché* (market) for produce, chatting up the sellers, is a lovely morning activity. They buy fresh flowers for their homes weekly, not only on special occasions. They stop for a coffee with a friend after dropping kids off at school and before heading to work. They take leisurely lunches and might even have a glass of wine if they feel like it. Many Frenchies love walking through the flea market on a Saturday or Sunday to dig through antiques, searching for mix-and-match porcelain plates or crystal glassware. When they join with friends and family at a table, it's beautifully set with all the different pieces they have found, the better for enjoying long, even epic, multi-course meals when conversation might revolve around wine, travels, and history. Rarely do they talk about work.

No matter if we're in Paris or at home, we all want to live the good life. You know, the kind of life that doesn't always feel rushed. When you savor small moments such as sitting in a manicured garden brimming with fragrant flowers or enjoying

Parisians find joy in what they eat, where they go, conversations they have, and how they spend their time. Simple things. It's their North Star.

a long, leisurely lunch with wine, cheese, *and* dessert. When you feel pride for who you are, or who you have become, because keeping up, showing off, or being perfect just isn't necessary. When you explore and find things or places that charm you or bring you little jolts of bright-eyed wonder—be it an antique jewelry box, a cute little town, or a buttery, flaky croissant. The kind of life that is full of *joie*—joy—every day, not just when you're on vacation.

When a French friend asked me how I could possibly write about the French's joie de vivre when they can be a grumpy bunch who complain and strike all the time, I admit I didn't have the answer right away. I hadn't quite put it into words, but after more than a decade of living in France, I have come to understand how different joy is from happiness. Happiness is a state of being. It is surface level, immediate, and can be fleeting: The sun is out and I'm leaving for vacation tomorrow; I am happy in this moment. Joy, on the other hand, is something deeper, less vulnerable to the inevitable ebbs and flows of daily life. In other words, you might not be happy, but you can still access joy. If that doesn't sound like the French, then I don't know what does!

After living in France—amongst its *joie*-seekers, I have found that kind of enjoyable life—the good life. A life that brings me pleasures in very simple things, strengthens my connections with the people around me, and elicits deep satisfaction in myself and my desires. This kind of joy isn't reserved for the elite. You don't have to have grown up in a family with money or privilege. I didn't. And you don't have to have deep pockets. I don't. Anyone can access *joie* anywhere they live, and no matter who they are. It's not even about buying things, really. It's about experiencing moments. It's about noticing feelings. It's about appreciating the *why* and the *how* much more than the *who*, *what*, *when*, and *where*.

As a Nigerian raised in Austin, Texas, I never imagined that I'd one day be living what one would call "the good life." I thought the best things in life were reserved for ultra-wealthy and affluent people. I grew up thinking if you were lucky enough to have something special or fancy, you saved it and didn't dare use it daily.

In May of 2020, I wrote a blog post for my lifestyle brand Madame de la Maison called "A Case for the Good China," which resonated with a lot of people. In the article, I shared how my Nigerian-Jamaican mother never wanted to use her best china for everyday meals or even with her favorite church buddies. She was waiting for a "special occasion," which sadly never came because she died when I was twelve; before she turned forty. In the days after I published the post (see "Do Use the Good China," page 155), readers flooded me with sweet messages and their own similar stories of how they don't use objects they love nearly as often as they'd like.

Readers connected strongly with my post because no one wants to miss out on using "the good china," which for me has become a metaphor for living our best lives and sharing experiences and rituals that we find beautiful and that bring us moments of joy. Everyone has a bucket list of things they want to do someday that will somehow enrich their life. Not to knock the beloved bucket, but why not strive to find fulfillment and joy every day, starting now? And damn it, why be like my mother and wait for a special occasion to pull the good china out of the cabinet? We deserve to experience joy every day.

Since moving to France in 2011, I have come to realize that finding joy in my everyday life is a value that I, too, have always deeply desired. It's what led me to beg my mother to let us eat off of her white floral porcelain instead of plastic Tupperware. I moved here, to Paris, as a career-obsessed, conspicuous consumption–loving New Yorker who was never satisfied and was always looking for ways to be happier and richer. Adapting to a different pace and way of life by learning from French culture has inspired and changed me in infinite ways. *Joie* has become my guiding principle, too.

It also led me to launch my business, Madame de la Maison, a lifestyle brand that encourages people to use beautiful objects like antiques and linens to help elevate moments around the table to celebrate every day, connect with others, and create pleasurable memories. And we can do all of this away from the table as well.

It is in that same spirit that I wanted to write this book, which is full of lessons I have learned from French culture. In focusing on five key areas—leisure, food and wine, gathering, beauty around you, and your own well-being—I share with you a little bit of my story, and how I came to learn these lessons, which sometimes (read: most times) meant making a fool of myself. My goal is to encourage you to live mindfully, seek out beauty, and celebrate life's joys, whether big or small.

I have become a Parisian, but I know that life differs slightly if you live in the countryside or even other cities of France. I also know that I cannot generalize a population of people. I can, however, share my observations, insights from fellow Parisians who live the good life, and some fascinating history and inspiration that have influenced me while living here. To me, these lessons are worthy of sharing so that others might benefit wherever they are in the world.

The French don't always get everything right, but going back centuries and still today, theirs is a culture that celebrates appreciating the little things and finding beauty all around us. Perhaps now more than ever, we all could use a little help discovering joy in the everyday, wherever and in whatever circumstances we find ourselves. Cheers to the Good Life!

ON SLOWING DOWN

LEARN TO FIND
PLEASURE IN JUST BEING

Below

Stroll with a friend down the Quai des Célestins to the perfect perch spot on Île Saint-Louis.

Opposite

The fountain in the garden of the Palais-Royal where you can lounge in chairs and people watch.

What has struck me so far chiefly is the absolute laziness of everybody over here. When do these people work? What do they work at? People here seem to have established an elaborate system of loafing. I don't understand it at all.

—Thomas Edison, 1889, on Paris

THE ART
OF *ÊTRE*

Without my even knowing it, my first visit to Paris—a single day of aimlessly wandering around on my own as a naïve but curious twenty-something—taught me one of the most essential lessons in embracing life as the French do: *l'art d'être,* or "the art of being." Even my getting to Paris was itself on par with the laissez-faire attitude the French are known for: I was studying abroad in London when I decided to take advantage of its proximity to France to visit Paris for the day. I couldn't think of anything more exciting or glamorous.

With only two semesters' worth of French 101 semi-ingrained in my brain and no itinerary, I hopped on a train one summer morning without a plan. This was before smartphones, social media, or GPS. I didn't want to spend the little money I had on a guidebook, so I decided that a free map from the station would have to do. The goal was just to *loaf,* a term that has nothing to do with bread and everything to do with wandering the day away, taking it all in, and then bragging to everyone back home that "*Ooh la la,* I visited Paris!"

At the time, I wasn't even a Francophile—and I had no reason to be. While I was growing up in Texas, my Jamaican and Nigerian family only ever talked about helping relatives immigrate to the States to fulfill the American Dream. The idea of moving anywhere else was a concept for the movies, not for us. I also wasn't particularly well-read at the time—unless you count the glossy pages of fashion magazines. These taught me that only wealthy and stylish people visited Paris to shop, attend runway shows, and continue just being fabulous.

I didn't know that African Americans like Josephine Baker, Nina Simone, and James Baldwin had escaped to Paris to find freedom from the segregation and racism they experienced in the United States. I hadn't yet dog-eared a copy of Ernest Hemingway's *A Moveable Feast,* so I couldn't have known that Paris is a place that stays with you for the rest of your life. Nor had I underlined parts of a translated copy of Louis-Sébastien Mercier's nineteenth-century treatise *Tableau de Paris,* in which he writes, "It has been said that one has to breathe the air of Paris to achieve perfection of any sort . . . If I am not mistaken, Paris' air must have something special in it."

Still, though unprepared, I unknowingly transformed myself into a modern-day flâneur—or, as a woman, a *flâneuse*—the nineteenth-century term for anyone who wanders around idly while observing people and their surroundings. (More on the flâneur on page 19.) To loaf like a local, I attempted to camouflage myself in a black tank top, jeans, and stretchy platform sandals. Then I devoured the city in what turned out to be an unforgettable, life-changing experience.

Opposite
Perfectly lined trees in the Palais-Royal.

These are the kind of moments that often inspire some of the essential ingredients of joy—curiosity, creativity, connection, celebration.

From Gare du Nord, I walked down the Canal Saint-Martin, where people sat outside bars in those iconic rattan chairs sipping their morning café with a newspaper. From there, I strolled from one arrondissement to another, looking in the windows of cheese shops, bakeries, and *caves,* which I'd later learn were where one shopped for wine. There were specialty stores devoted to specific types of literature, antiques, and artisanal stationery and even a windowful of broken dolls—which was borderline creepy, but I also liked that there could be a shop for something so niche.

As I walked, I inhaled the unmistakable scent of butter, only to indulge my senses further with a flaky, buttery croissant. Somehow, I found my way to the gardens of Place des Vosges, where elegant elders sat on benches engaged in deep conversation, small children giggled and ran around screeching, and lovers lay close together in the grass stroking a forehead, moving aside strands of hair, and kissing as if the world weren't watching. I observed many generations in one beautiful space surrounded by centuries-old architecture I knew nothing about at the time. In an effort to pass the time luxuriously, and see if I could listen in on the conversations going on around me, I plopped myself down on the grass, undeterred by my inability to understand French.

Next, I headed down the rue de Rivoli to have lunch at a café. I looked for familiar items on the menu, ones I might have encountered in my high school French textbook, and settled on a croque monsieur. Then I proudly ordered a glass of white wine. Back home, I was still underage, so this small act felt deviant and divine. I sat on the café's *terrasse*—what the French call the patio space on the sidewalk—eating my croque and daydreaming about whether this was really what daily life in Paris was like.

After lunch, I cut over to the luxury shops of rue Saint-Honoré for some *lèche-vitrine*—a term that, to my amusement, translates literally to "window licking," but actually means "window shopping." Next, because I couldn't afford a ticket into the Louvre, I put my feet up on a bench in the nearby Jardin des Tuileries and thought about all the art inside that museum. I could see the tall tip of the Eiffel Tower peeking at me over the trees, so I walked along the Seine toward the only monument I recognized, stared up at it, took it all in, then bought a cheap souvenir key chain before heading back to the train station.

On the two-hour ride back to London that night, I looked out the train window, replaying all that had happened that day. It wasn't much—and yet, it was everything. I hadn't had a checklist or an agenda, but I had fully experienced the city in a sensorial way that only unplanned wandering can provide.

At the end of that summer, I returned to my university life in Fort Worth, Texas, and after graduating three years later, I moved to New York City to start a career in fashion. Those years in New York were all about "doing" and "having." Working as an editor and stylist in the fashion industry there was all-consuming. My days were filled with photo shoots and appointments, and my evenings with parties. I worked around the clock to advance both my career and my status. The cruel irony was that jobs in fashion weren't even well paid and didn't allow me to afford or enjoy the very lifestyle I was helping to sell. Yet, I attached my self-esteem to what I did for a living. I wasn't truly happy, though, and I rarely found moments of joy that weren't attached to an agenda. I always felt unsatisfied and didn't know how to *just be* . . . anything or anyone or anywhere. I'd entirely forgotten the lessons I'd learned that day in Paris.

After five years of styling shoots for magazines, I decided to get a master's degree in decorative arts at Bard Graduate Center. The program took me to Paris at the end of my first year for a summer intensive class. My classmates and I visited museums and gardens and walked the streets looking for evidence of past art movements. After that summer course, I stayed a few extra months to work on my master's thesis on the designer Jean Patou, in which I applied the German concept of *Gesamtkunstwerk,* or "total work of art," to show how interiors and fashion can represent a life we want to live. I returned to the fashion industry in New York after my research. Nine months later—at which point I had given up the idea of a life in Paris—I met a dashing Swiss German man on a video production job during Fashion Week.

He and I worked side by side for a long, exhausting week, yet he was so charming and calm in the midst of it all that I fell for him. Once the job was complete, he changed his flight and stayed in New York for an extra weekend, allowing us to enjoy the city and get to know each other in a more personal way. We strolled Central Park, lingered over glasses of wine at restaurants in Brooklyn, and talked for hours. Eventually, he went back to Paris, where he lived. But after nine months of long-distance dating, a handful of transatlantic flights, and countless video phone calls, we were engaged before the end of the year and then married the following.

And so, eleven years after that first trip, I returned to Paris. This time I was attached to someone else, yet I was still entirely independent and more intent than ever on exploring and celebrating *être* (being) as opposed to prioritizing *faire* (doing) or *avoir* (having). In a city seemingly conceived to inspire daydreaming—with its countless cafés, parks, cobblestone streets, grand architecture, and hidden corners—I learned to loaf.

I have tried not only to appreciate these idle moments when they come, but also to seek them out, to make space for them in my day, to know their value in a balanced and fulfilling rhythm of life. These are the kind of moments that often inspire some of the essential ingredients of joy— curiosity, creativity, connection, celebration.

And now, here I am, encouraging you to do the same. It's not always easy, but the returns, both seen and unseen, can be wonderfully rewarding. On your next vacation, give yourself at least one day without a plan. Spend a few hours just wandering around a city or give yourself permission to sit in a park or a café and *just be.*

WHAT'S A FLÂNEUR, ANYWAY?

Little did I know it at the time, but I was practicing the fine French art of *flânerie*—"wandering," or "strolling," or "dawdling." Or, rather, in proper French, I was a flâneur.

So, what, exactly, is a flâneur? Essentially, it's someone who loafs about, who roams without a purpose *on purpose*. The term itself was coined in the nineteenth century and was originally used to describe only the well-heeled—but in a way that eschews someone who has nothing better to do with their time. However, it has since been praised, and embraced, by various visitors and locals, from the famous to the obscure and from the nouveau riche to the bohemian artist. Now anyone can be a flâneur.

Jean-Jacques Rousseau, Honoré de Balzac, Charles Baudelaire—all three boasted of being flâneurs before the term itself was even coined. To wit, in 1790, Rousseau wrote:

Never have I thought so much, never have I realised my own existence so much, been so much alive, been so much myself . . . as in those journeys which I have made alone and afoot. Walking has something in it which animates and heightens my ideas: I can scarcely think when I stay in one place; my body must be set a-going if my mind is to work. The sight of the country, the succession of beautiful scenes . . . releases my soul, gives me greater courage of thought, throws me as it were into the midst of the immensity of the objects of Nature . . . my heart, surveying one object after another, unites itself, identifies itself with those in sympathy with it, surrounds itself with delightful images, intoxicates itself with emotions the most exquisite.

So, what do you need to hold the title of flâneur? Well, for one thing you don't need to wait for your next trip to Paris. With only a few basic things, you, too, can be a flâneur. You just need a pair of comfortable shoes, a sense of curiosity, and not a plan or care in the world.

Opposite
The gardens and covered walkways of the Palais–Royal.

Go out for a walk. It doesn't have to be a romantic walk in the park, spring at its most spectacular moment, flowers and smells and outstanding poetical imagery smoothly transferring you into another world. It doesn't have to be a walk during which you'll have multiple life epiphanies and discover meanings no other brain ever managed to encounter. Do not be afraid of spending quality time by yourself. Find meaning or don't find meaning but "steal" some time and give it freely and exclusively to your own self. Opt for privacy and solitude. That doesn't make you antisocial or cause you to reject the rest of the world. But you need to breathe. And you need to be.

—*Albert Camus,*
Notebooks, 1951–1959

Below
A stop at a café after strolling an ephemeral flea market in the Place des Vosges.

Opposite
La Brasserie de l'Isle Saint–Louis has a perfect view of the Quais de la Seine and the river.

To stroll is a science, it is the gastronomy of the eye. To walk is to vegetate, to stroll is to live . . . To stroll is to enjoy, it is to assume a mind-set, it is to admire the sublime pictures of unhappiness, of love, of joy, of graceful or grotesque portraits; it is to plunge one's vision to the depths of a thousand existences: young, it is to desire everything; old, it is to live the life of the young, to marry their passions."

—*Honoré de Balzac*

LOAFING IN PARIS

Paris is full of lovely places to loiter, linger, loaf, idly wander, or engage in whatever other leisurely behavior you desire. Here are a few of my favorites:

MONTMARTRE (1) is a hilltop neighborhood in the 18th arrondissement. It's well known as the home to artists like Henri Toulouse-Lautrec and Vincent van Gogh, who took up residence amid its crooked cobblestoned streets and ivy-covered iron gates. Popular movies like *Amélie* have made it a pilgrimage destination, but unless you're dead-set on finding the café where Amélie worked (Café des Deux Moulins at 15 rue Lepic), Montmartre is the perfect neighborhood to allow yourself to get lost meandering up and down its winding streets (like rue Lepic, rue Gabrielle, and rue Drevet) or peeking in the windows of the houses in the Villa Léandre. You will find cute cafés, stairs to sit down on, and tiny gardens with benches for perching as long as you want.

ÎLE SAINT-LOUIS (2) and **ÎLE DE LA CITÉ** (3) are two centrally situated islands in the 4th arrondissement smack-dab in the middle of the Seine. Both can be reached by bridges (Pont Neuf, most notably, for Île de la Cité), each with its own charm. Beyond the famous Notre Dame Cathedral, Île de la Cité is also home to the Préfecture de Police (the head police station, where we expats go for our visas), to an outdoor flower and bird market for your leisurely perusal, to the picture-perfect Place Dauphine for feeling like you're on a movie set, and to Square du Vert Galant for picnics. Île Saint-Louis is slightly less "full," but no less worthy, as it's home to the ice-cream parlor Berthillon (get the *caramel beurre salé*) and Square Barye, which is really more of a triangle at the tip of the island, facing east.

WALKING ALONG THE SEINE (4), the river that runs through Paris, dividing it into two banks, or *rives* (Rive Droite and Rive Gauche), is a quintessential pastime of which both locals and tourists partake. There are many areas along both sides of the Seine, with cleared pathways to walk, run, and even picnic on deserted patches of grass or concrete; while dangling your legs over the edges of the *quai*. I particularly enjoy walking down along the river on the Right Bank from the Pont du Sully until I can see the medieval Conciergerie, where Marie Antoinette spent her final days.

My favorite pastime is letting
time pass by, having time,
taking time, wasting time, living
out of time.

—*Françoise Sagan*

CANAL SAINT-MARTIN (5) and its northern neighbor the **BASSIN DE LA VILLETTE** are a bit less known to tourists, but they're both worth a wander for a real slice of Parisian life—in particular among the *bobo* (bourgeois bohemian) set, who, in summer, sprawl on either side of the canal with drinks and takeaway snacks from nearby spots like Siseng and Gros Bao. Once you hit the Jaurès Métro station, brace yourself for a bit of chaos at the roundabout before continuing along the wider part of the canal. This section will take you all the way up to the Parc de la Villette, which is full of green spaces for picnics or outdoor movies, amusement park rides, playgrounds, concert halls, and more. It's a real "Wow, I didn't know this existed" part of Paris.

THE TUILERIES (6) is home to the quintessentially Paris green chairs and is close to Pierre Hermé, one of my favorite places to get ice cream in the summer. The Tuileries is such a large park, so there are ample spots to picnic, lie on a blanket, run, or just waltz around staring at the architecture and statues. Plus, people-watching is great, too, as you really get a mix of visitors—be they tourists, editors in town for Fashion Week, locals on a run, or lovers on a date.

THE PALAIS-ROYAL (7)—which, as its name suggests, was once a residence for visiting kings and queens—is surprisingly hidden. You'd never know it was there unless you were looking for it, and then, next thing you know, you're inside this rectangle lined with perfectly manicured trees, high-end boutiques, and historical bistros like Le Grand Véfour. (Yes, the one featured in Woody Allen's *Midnight in Paris;* Le Grand Colbert, just around the corner, was also featured in *Something's Gotta Give.*) It's the perfect place to pause.

LE MARCHÉ AUX PUCES DE SAINT-OUEN (8) is a must for wandering, even if you're not buying (a rarity for me!). It's located north of Paris, just outside the ring road (or *périphérique*)—specifically check out the **VERNAISON** and **PAUL BERT SERPETTE** markets. Vernaison is this amazing labyrinth of antique treasures, and Paul Bert Serpette is more organized (and pricier) but full of inspiration.

A CHAT WITH A PARISIAN FLÂNEUR

FRANK BARRON
American in Paris, baker, and author of
*Sweet Paris: Seasonal Recipes from an
American Baker in France*

I followed Frank online for a few years and, like
so many others, was mesmerized by his sweet
concoctions and his photos of Paris. We were
finally set up on a friend date and have been
meeting up in cafés across the city ever since. The
first thing I noticed about Frank was how well he
dressed for someone who spent his days walking
all over the city café-hopping. But that's Frank:
always put together and always up for a chat and a
good wander—which is why I asked him about his
flâneur habits.

Q: Tell me about your flâneur philosophy in Paris.

A: I am inspired by the lovely Diana Vreeland,
who said, "The eye has to travel." And I'm a
firm believer in that as well, which encapsulates
my philosophy. Being a flâneur is going out and
eating everything with your eyes and being open
to new experiences, but also to all of the crazy
around us. When I am walking, I am constantly
looking for details; and as a lover of all things
beautiful, I am constantly inspired by Paris. It's
one giant outdoor museum and such a perfect
backdrop for all of the flâneurs out there.

Q: Is it different when you travel? How do you
implement your philosophy on the road?

A: When I travel to a new place that I haven't
visited before, it just gets totally dialed up.
There's still things I'm inspired by every day in
Paris, even after ten years of living here, but when
I go to a new city, all of a sudden things become
more electric. I feel more excitement, waking up
in the morning, to go out and really see what,
let's say, Venice, has to offer. That's another city
with an amazing backdrop for flâneurs to literally
stroll the canals of Venice and just eat up all those
gorgeous details. Most people, when they travel,
they're excited to go out and discover specific
things they've read or been told about, and I think
that's the brilliance of being a flâneur: You put
away your guidebook and put away your phone
and sort of just get lost. The fun is not knowing
where you're going to wind up.

Q: What is your favorite neighborhood, street, or area to walk?

A: Definitely around the Palais-Royal area. I'm there almost every day. I ride my bike over there, park it, and walk all around. It's one of my favorite gardens in the whole city. I love going there as the season changes to spring, to watch the magnolias come out. Even though it's a well-trodden path for me, and I've been there millions of times, I still find beauty and inspiration whenever I go. And I usually see something that I haven't seen before. I love the Japanese quarter, too. I'm very inspired by walking up and down rue Sainte-Anne. I feel transported to Tokyo while being in the center of Paris. You see these beautiful Parisian buildings and doors, yet there's mochi bars, Japanese tea cafés, and you can get a matcha latte everywhere. These are places I could keep going back to over and over again and still have a different, dreamy experience every time.

Q: Do you have any special tools for wandering?

A: My two favorite accessories for wandering are a newspaper, generally the international *New York Times* and, of course, my dog, Fitzgerald.

Q: Comfortable walking shoes/sneakers, or suffer for fashion while walking?

A: Suffer for fashion, *bien sûr*.

Q: Do you prefer to *flâner* solo or with someone?

A: Well, minus the dog, I always prefer to wander solo, which makes it a lot easier to strike up those conversations with a stranger, whether in a café or sitting on a park bench. Part of the joy of flâneuring is that you never know who you're going to chat up, bump into, or what the city will put in front of you.

Q: What's the most magical or unexpected discovery you've made while wandering?

A: On my last trip to Japan, I remember one afternoon of aimlessly strolling the streets of Gion, in Kyoto. I wandered into a side street and discovered an open gate that led to a courtyard temple flanked by cherry blossom trees with not a soul in sight. It felt like I had discovered a portal to another, more magical era.

Q: What tips do you have for the nouveau flâneur?

A: Saunter, stroll, and savor with intention. Open your eyes to the quiet beauty of the details around you.

A CHAT WITH A PARISIAN FLÂNEUSE

VANESSA GRALL
French American in Paris, founder of Messy Nessy Chic, and author of *Don't Be a Tourist in Paris* and *Don't Be a Tourist in New York*

Since moving to Paris, I have been a follower and devoted reader of Messy Nessy Chic, the online "cabinet of chic curiosities" helmed by Vanessa Grall, a modern-day *flâneuse* whose explorations led to the creation of her full-time business. In fact, her newsletters helped me discover the most interesting bits of history in this city and inspired many adventures to unknown corners. Vanessa knows Paris like the back of her hand, but she is also a keen observer of and commentator on the quirks of its inhabitants.

Q: What is your flâneur philosophy?

A: My number one rule is to always look up, especially in Paris, which is basically an open museum for architecture. But I've also found myself looking down a lot, too, because I've been really lucky with my office balcony, which overlooks the market square in the Latin Quarter. I love people-watching. And, actually, I think the most enjoyable part of being a flâneur is observing and appreciating those around us—imagining the stories of strangers and finding compassion and beauty in our fellow humans. People-watching helps restore my faith in humanity on a daily basis. Essentially, that's what Baudelaire was doing: traveling the city and watching people.

Q: Speaking of traveling, does your flâneur philosophy change when you leave Paris?

A: My philosophy when I travel is to rediscover the personal joy of travel; follow your instincts, not the tour buses. We forget how to be mindful of our own individual interests and passions. My secret recipe is to go with your mood. My whole book is structured around that idea, rather than being organized by activity or area. Take your own interests and frame of mind into account when you're discovering new places. Also, talk to locals! The waiters, the shopkeepers, the old guy sitting next to you at the bar—ask them questions.

Q: What is your favorite neighborhood, street, or area to walk in Paris?

A: I'm still excited when I find a street that I've never been down. It's like entering a new little world every time. It helps me get a better picture of the past. Like, I knew Montparnasse, but I just realized after twelve years that there's a huge concentration of incredible art nouveau architecture around the Montparnasse Cemetery. Oh, and speaking of cemeteries, I love Père Lachaise, in the 20th arrondissement in Paris's City of the Dead. It sounds creepy, but Père Lachaise's winding cobblestone pathways all have their own street signs, and the tombs look like small Gothic houses. Jim Morrison, Edith Piaf, and Oscar Wilde are a few of the many famous people buried there. It's like a miniature city full of history, Parisian folklore, and mystery.

Opposite
Vanessa Grall flipping through art at the *bouquinistes* along the Seine.

Q: Let's talk tools for wandering. What do you bring with you?

A: My Mobylette, a vintage pedal-start moped. You can go further afield in Paris, park it, and then start wandering around back streets and getting lost. It helps me cover more ground.

Q: What about comfortable walking shoes or sneakers? Or, do you suffer for fashion while you're walking?

A: If I'm alone, with no one to slow me down, I can keep wandering until my feet are aching. So, yes, comfortable walking shoes. For me, it's Natural World Moccasins, a French closet staple.

Q: Do you prefer to *flâner* solo or with someone?

A: Well, my husband, Alex, showed me Paris when we first met and I had just moved here from London. I saw it from the back of his scooter. Today, I love our Sunday strolls. But I also think my best wandering is when I'm solo—just because of my stamina or obsessiveness and because I don't want to miss anything. But now I have two children, and I'm really curious to see if one or both of them will enjoy wandering around, too.

Q: What are the most magical or unexpected discoveries you've made while wandering?

A: There are so many, and every time I find one, I have to write about it. However, I'd say, maybe the weirdest one was when I found an old Belle Époque theater that's hiding inside a discount shoe store in [the *quartier*] Barbès. That was an eye-opening moment. Driving through the 11th arrondissement one day, I stopped because I was curious about this insanely giant door and peeked in to find one of Paris's last prop houses, Lanzani. It's like Aladdin's cave of wonders. Being a flâneur in the catacombs is also pretty surreal.

Q: Can you share three of your top flâneur spots?

A: The Marché Vernaison is my favorite spot to wander around. The tiny little alleyways feel like a maze. I also love strolling the Seine, which is like Paris's highway of activity. You can always find a fellow flâneur browsing the *bouquinistes,* the little open-air bookshops along the river. Another favorite would definitely be the city's hidden network of covered passageways— Galerie Vivienne, Passage des Panoramas, Passage Verdeau, et cetera—all built in the Belle Époque to provide refuge from the bustling streets. And they were technically the world's first indoor shopping malls, lined with elegant shops and little eateries. Back in the day, they also had small theaters, reading rooms, and public baths. They were definitely the stomping ground of flâneurs and elegant dandies. Today, under the same glass roofs, the merchant spirit is still there. They're still selling their books, old photographs, and bric-a-brac. It's perfect for a rainy day and a pretty nice alternative to a traditional shopping mall.

Opposite
Looking through the books and old posters at the *bouquinistes* along the Seine is one of Vanessa's favorite spots to *flâner.*

CAFÉ LIFE IS A GOOD LIFE

When my daughter turned three, the legal age when kids begin school in France, and started *maternelle* (preschool), I was excited to leave her in good hands bright and early and then zip back to my desk. But once I dropped her off, I found myself making my way through a crowd of adults chatting in the school's courtyard and the sidewalk out front. I looked around and thought, *Damn, don't these people have stuff to do? It's eight thirty* A.M. *You know where your kids are, so get to work!* But even when the weather turned cold, the other parents still lingered nearby, squeezing like sausages into the tiny café next door to the school to catch up before rushing off. They were in no hurry. After a few weeks of confused observation, however, I quickly became *jalouse*. I began to appreciate that these French parents didn't share my anxiety; they weren't running off to work early in the morning. They knew they deserved thirty minutes or so to catch up with friends before starting their day. It took a few months, but I finally started nudging my way into the same routine.

I don't always stop or stay for a coffee, but I do loiter around the front of the school a bit longer before heading back to my showroom, aka my living room. When I get home, I put on a kettle, pour myself tea in a lovely antique cup, and sit with a book or a magazine (or sometimes my to-do list) for about twenty minutes. The idea is to move slowly into my day, rather than jumping in feverishly, and I can thank the parents of the Parisian schoolyard for teaching me this. It took a lot less convincing for me to get into the *apéro* (see "Happy Hour À La Française," page 109) that magically materializes following after-school pickup when it's warm out. The kids get a *sirop* with water or an Orangina, while we adults order a beer or wine.

When it was announced that France's schools and cafés would close during the 2020 lockdown in the face of Covid-19, I remember that last, sad walk to the café with the other parents. Once there, we pushed tables together, sat down, and solemnly discussed how we would manage. I didn't realize how much I had come to rely on this ritual until the café reopened after nine months. That first day back, I spent hours with friends on the terrace of Le Nemours, near the Palais-Royal, in the 1st arrondissement. (Le Nemours is a great spot to people-watch, even when it's raining, because you can sit under the beautiful grand arches.) When I spoke about the lockdown with a man sitting nearby, he broke down in tears. In France, he said, sitting among others in a café was essential to life and to joie de vivre.

Opposite
Catching up with a friend over tea at La Fontaine de Belleville near the Canal Saint-Martin.

Obviously, I am not alone in my devotion to café culture, which has a long and well-documented history and is a central part of Paris's identity. Since the seventeenth century, cafés in Paris have been a gathering place and a center for social life for the working class and artist crowd. The café is a place you go to occupy space and connect with other people—whether you talk to them or not. In the nineteenth century, Mercier wrote that the café was "the ordinary refuge of the idler and the shelter of the indigent." Even if you are solo, there is a sense of connection in a café. There, lingering is welcomed, even encouraged.

My experience in coffee shops in the United States had consisted largely of grabbing a latte in a paper cup and running off to my next destination. Occasionally, I would bring along my laptop and sit, but I don't remember feeling at ease nibbling on a muffin while the revolving door of patrons came and went with their disposable cups and brown bags of snacks to go.

Parisian café culture might just be one of my favorite things about life in France. Whether I want to meet a friend to catch up or organize a meeting to discuss a new project, the question is always "Hey, should we meet up for *un café*?" (*Café,* by the way, can also mean tea, wine, and nibbles.) Meetings aside, the café is where I go to kill time, to spend time, and to forget about time. It's a loafing lover's dream.

Opposite
You can order anything from wine to coffee to tea at the cafés in Paris and linger for hours.

While writing this book (and afterward), I frequented a few different cafés, including one near my kids' school, but the one I visited the most was close to my apartment. It's a neighborhood spot where locals and regulars stop in for lunch, coffee, or an alcoholic drink. I chose it for proximity and because it looked friendly. I usually show up around the same time as a select group of other local regulars. When each one walks in, they'll get the same hearty welcome from the owners that I received: *Salut! Ça va?* Even when customers aren't sharing tables, they'll shout over them and across the space—about food, politics, or just to joke around. I guess you can say the place has become my Cheers. Sometimes, while there, I'll see the owner of the nearby wine cellar, the cheesemonger, a friend from the area, other restaurant owners, or the owner of the nearby épicerie. The café is a community space where I can connect or just sit and let the good vibes flow through me. This is a moment and a space where I am almost guaranteed to feel joy. No matter how much actual work I get done, I have never left without feeling satisfied, content, and connected.

We can all learn something from Parisian café culture, a cherished tangible and intangible experience that can move a person to tears. While you might not live near a Parisian café, I encourage you to find a place that serves coffee in real cups, that offers food on proper plates, and that encourages lingering. Meet a friend there and occupy space to talk, connect, and exchange life experiences and ideas. Take a pause from busy days and takeout lunches.

CAFÉ ESSENTIALS

A typical Parisian café is full of loafers because it's the ideal place to do absolutely nothing (or everything), all with a glass, hot or cold, in hand. To properly loaf in a café as the French do, you should consider taking with you a few essential items. However, no matter what you bring or why you're there, there's no need to rush.

- **MAGAZINE OR BOOK:** Pick one with tattered edges—you don't actually have to read it; you can simply leave it open to give yourself the appearance of being very literary and intellectual.

- **PEN AND NOTEBOOK:** Sketch and/or write your next great work or capture the creative thoughts filling your mind from the comings and goings all around you.

- **LAPTOP:** A laptop is acceptable for writers, but slap yours shut when café o'clock becomes *apéro* o'clock.

- **SUNGLASSES:** If you're sitting out on the café *terrasse* (patio), wear these when the sun makes its way over to your side of the street and occasionally to hide your ogling of the outfit on the Parisienne sitting next to you.

- **CIGS:** These are for the puffers, but be prepared to get nasty looks when your smoke wafts over to your neighbor, who may be eating a burger at the same time.

- **NEWSPAPER:** Catch up on politics and strike up conversations about current events with people at the neighboring tables.

- **NOTHING AT ALL:** You won't be the only one whimsically gazing out on the world while enjoying your beverage.

Opposite
Le Nemours, one of my favorite cafés, is one of the best spots for people watching in the city.

CAFÉS IN PARIS

Sit on the terrace under the arches at **LE NEMOURS** (1), near the Palais-Royal; take a book to **LA FONTAINE DE BELLEVILLE** (2), where you won't be distracted by Wi-Fi. Take your tea inside the seemingly secret café at **JARDIN DU PETIT PALAIS** (3), get your Simone de Beauvoir on at one of the crammed-together tables at **CAFÉ DE FLORE** (4), and resist plotting your own heist à la the fictional gentleman thief Arsène Lupin at the Louvre from a table nestled under the arches of **LE CAFÉ MARLY** (5). Prepare to feel like you're on a movie set at **LA MAISON ROSE** (6) in Montmartre.

LADIES (AND GENTLEMEN) WHO LUNCH

Opposite

Restaurants, like Bonhomie in the 10th arrondissement, offer a prix fixe lunch menu.

For most of my adult working life, I have been a freelancer or worked for myself and from home. Come lunchtime, it's pretty common to find me slumped over my computer shoving salad leaves or the previous night's leftovers into my mouth while tapping away at my keyboard. It's a habit I formed while working in a big office as a fashion editor on 34th Street in Manhattan.

It wasn't until I moved to France that I realized the importance of the lunch break—*le pause déjeuner*. And, in fact, this sacred midday break has changed the rhythm of my days. I used to work through lunch and try to find something to eat at three P.M.–ish, when I finally realized I was hungry—only to discover that most restaurants in Paris were closed until dinner. (These strict hours are a bit looser for brasseries with nonstop service, but, generally, the window of opportunity for lunching in Paris is from about twelve noon to two P.M. (maybe two thirty, if you're lucky) or one thirty outside the city.

Even essential shops close so their employees can take a midday break—so, you can forget about doing errands instead. Double-checking operating hours is imperative in France. It took some time for me to understand the rigid timing and purpose of lunch, and even though I wasn't working in an office, I quickly learned that the midday break is something the French take seriously—so seriously that French labor law actually forbids workers from eating at their desks. It's a reminder that this culture values a work/life balance and that we are not meant to slavishly go, go, go around the clock.

I asked my friend Astrid, a Parisienne and a PR director for a large company, how big a deal lunch is at her office. I wanted to know if, perhaps, when she had an important deadline, she ate at her desk or skipped lunch. Her response? "Impossible." She would never eat in front of her computer or not take a lunch break. My friend Laura, a transplant to Paris from Lyon, who has worked at the same communications agency for fourteen years, echoed the same horror at the suggestion. *Jamais.* "Never." Lunch, Laura says, gives rhythm to one's day; there is before, and there is after. You work better in the morning knowing the break is coming, and you work better in the afternoon having taken that break.

French workers either go out to a brasserie or restaurant and enjoy two to three courses at lunch, or they grab takeaway and return to the office to sit at a *grand table,* where they eat all together, never alone at their desks. And there is zero talk of work. At Laura's office, anyone who brings up work gets immediately shushed with *Oh, no no no! C'est la pause.* During lunch break, there are many things to discuss, like weekend or travel plans, the cinema, the latest binge-worthy TV shows, new exhibitions, or family life—but never work.

Opposite
Le Chardenoux is a
classic French restaurant
for lunch or dinner with
beautiful interiors in the
11th arrondissement.

Astrid's office has a fancy canteen—known in French as a *restaurant enterprise* (which I learned is a selling point for companies to attract talent). Laura's partner, David, who, like me, has his own small business, uses lunchtime to catch up with friends at restaurants. He, too, would never dream of missing *la pause déjeuner* or enjoying it at a proper table.

Companies that don't have a canteen on-site will offer their employees a *ticket resto,* or "restaurant ticket," which looks like Monopoly money and is accepted at all restaurants. Can you imagine? A company that financially contributes to your lunch? What's more, nobody bats a judgmental eye if wine or beer is ordered. The café chalkboards that litter the sidewalks of Paris offer two to three courses from a *menu à prix fixe,* a "fixed-price menu," costing from sixteen to fifty euros. After having your starter, main dish, wine, and perhaps dessert, you can enjoy coffee or tea before getting the check and heading back to the office. I could never have fathomed sitting for a multi-course meal back in my New York City fashion magazine days, but French culture caters to this break.

Indoctrination in this idea starts young. At school, most children have ninety minutes for lunch and the option to eat it at home with their family. My daughter started coming home for lunch once a week at age seven. I once suggested that after we eat, she use the extra time to improve her reading. But she quickly reminded me that this was her break and went off to play until it was time to return to school. Knowing how to protect her moments of *être* is just one of the many ways in which she is undeniably French.

LUNCH LIKE THE FRENCH

It might be hard to break the habit of working through lunch, but these simple steps will help you reclaim your *pause déjeuner* and enjoy a nice serving of midday *joie*. Remember: You have many more hours to get stuff done. A well-deserved break will not only make you happier, but also allow you to see your work through rejuvenated eyes.

STEP 1. When the clock strikes noon, back away from your work.

STEP 2. Find a restaurant with a prix fixe menu or, if you are bringing lunch from home, a sunny park bench.

STEP 3. Meet with a friend to catch up or make a solo date with yourself to decompress. Maybe even leave your phone behind.

STEP 4. Let yourself have a glass of wine if you so desire.

STEP 5. Savor every course by putting your fork down between bites.

STEP 6. Don't think or talk about work. If your mind wanders to unpleasant or stressful issues, take a deep breath.

STEP 7. Read a book or a magazine if you are alone. Or, simply look around.

Above
All around Paris you will see chalkboard signs advertising a lunch prix fixe menu with entrée, plat, and dessert.

Opposite
Sometimes dessert is just a cheese plate and a little fruit.

HOLIDAYS ARE HOLY DAYS

Growing up, I always had two and a half months off from school for summer vacation. But my dad worked full time as an economist for the state of Texas, and my mother, who studied to be a botanist, ended up working seasonally at the Internal Revenue Service, so they didn't have many vacation days. My parents were also devout Christians and had been taught to work hard and provide for their family, which meant that my feisty Jamaican grandmother kept us kids equally busy during our summer break. That verse from Proverbs about idle hands being the devil's workshop? My grandmother took those words pretty seriously. She'd even create fake schoolwork for us, followed by sewing, reading, and exercise, before sending us off to pick peaches from a neighbor's tree. Rest, for all of us, would be rewarded in heaven.

Similarly, many Americans tend to see time as money and are less inclined to take time off that could be spent working, competing, or climbing the corporate ladder. And when they are on vacation, many have a hard time disconnecting. Calls still get answered, emails get checked. Why is it so hard for Americans to slow down and fully accept what days off are meant for?

The French, for their part, treat vacation—*les vacances*—like a religion. It's no wonder many often use the British term *holidays* to describe them. For the French, these are actual *holy days* and should be treated as such. In fact, the French subscribe to, and talk obsessively about, their *vacances scolaires* (school holidays), *les grands vacances* and the *fermeture annuelle* (summer break), and even the little mini-breaks throughout the year called *les ponts* (or "bridges," because they fall before or after a weekend, allowing people to "create a bridge" for a longer break). When I meet Parisians for the first time, I often hear about their vacation plans or desires before I learn what they do for a living. For so many, their jobs don't define them, and their identities are rarely tied up in their professional status. (This explains why it's considered rude in France to ask someone early in a relationship or conversation what they do for work.) For the French, a job is a means to an end.

Opposite

From late July through the end of August, shopkeepers display handwritten signs stating the boutique's closure, and the sign usually ends with a message from the team wishing you a beautiful summer.

LE FLÂNEUR

CUISINE à base de produits frais   CAFÉ-BISTROT   APÉR

WORK TO LIVE, DON'T LIVE TO WORK

Most of my French friends start planning their summer holidays—what the French call *les grands vacances*—six months in advance. At first, I found this a bit aggressive. But I soon realized that there's joy derived in spending the gray winter days planning what you will do in summer. It gives you something to look forward to and, of course, talk about with everyone when sharing ideas for future trips. Plus, if you wait until the last minute—as I have foolishly done—almost all the hotels, resorts, and *gîtes* (holiday cottages) will be booked up, and that's no way to start your fun.

Vacation—or "holy days"—should be a time for you and your loved ones to unplug, rest, recharge, discover, explore . . . Fill in the blank with anything else that's not work. Even my kids know this. While I may buy them a *cahier de vacances* (vacation notebook) filled with educational activities, to encourage them to do a little schoolwork over the summer—as my grandma did with me—they always remind me that these are *their* holy days, too, and the notebooks remain mostly empty by the end of summer. They aren't wrong. In fact, not only do I think it's wonderful that kids have so much time off in France, but I like that, from a young age, they begin to find pleasure in leisure.

Above
Playing cards on vacation in Fontvieille, Provence.

Opposite
Strolling around Oppède le Vieux, Provence.

Tip

If you vacation in July, you are a juilletiste; *if in August, an* aoûtien. *Our family is comprised mostly of* aoûtiens—*but we like to dip our toes in* juilletiste *territory from time to time.*

THE RIGHT
TO RELAX

For a long time, only the French aristocracy and
the bourgeoisie got days off to rest and relax.
But in 1936, France became the first European
country to pass a law requiring all companies to
offer two weeks of paid vacation, which meant
the working class could finally enjoy extended
moments to rest with no threat to their pay or
livelihood.

Today, French law guarantees five weeks of
paid vacation and up to eleven weeks for those
who work more than thirty-five hours a week, in
addition to the eleven national holidays sprinkled
throughout the year. (In May, there is a holiday
almost every single week!) What's more, about
80 percent of French people don't go very far to
spend their summer holidays—they tend to stay
in France.

In 2018, France passed another law, called
the *droit à la déconnexion,* which serves as a healthy
reminder for employees and their employers that
everyone has the "right to disconnect," meaning
your boss can't contact you during off hours or
vacation to ask you for anything.

In August, Paris is a ghost town, with
restaurants, bakeries, and even dry cleaners
closing for the entire month. Some locals love
it and prepare for it. They get all they need
beforehand, take note of who will be open in
their quartier, and revel in being one of the few
neighbors who hasn't fled for *la plage* (the beach).
Most shopkeepers slap handwritten signs on their
windows, close shop for a month, and head off
for vacation. (A word of advice: I wouldn't rely
on Google to find out if a place is open, as many
shopkeepers and businesses don't keep their
listings updated.) I enjoy reading these signs,
whose messages range from "just the facts" to
clever riddles.

*Opposite (clockwise
from top left)*
Robion; Roussillon;
Ambiose in the Loire
Valley; Menton.

A CASE FOR THE WEEKEND RETREAT

Opposite

Maison Ceronne in Le Perche is a country-chic and design lover's dream about two and a half hours from Paris by car.

Whether or not you live in France, when you have a break—even if it's just a Saturday or a Sunday—take it! And I mean, truly savor it. Make your own "right to disconnect" law and plan your break ahead of time, so you have something to look forward to.

My French friend Laura is the queen of planning quick trips for our parents' group— and she does it super far in advance. One year, she organized a September weekend getaway to Giverny for four families (six adults and six kids) and a big birthday trip to Provence for a group of twenty friends. The best was when she urged us to commit to a May weekend at Maison Ceronne, in Le Perche, where we sang karaoke and just loafed for two days straight.

There is so much you can do with a weekend and a variety of ways to extend those two days into slightly longer retreats without using too many vacation days. This is where *les ponts* (bridges) come in. For example, if Thursday is a public holiday—think of Thanksgiving in the States—you *faire le pont* to Saturday by taking Friday off, and— *voilà!* Four-day weekend! If Friday is a public holiday, you take Thursday off and—four-day weekend! Most Americans are already keen to this concept, what with the likes of one-day public observances such as Presidents' Day, Martin Luther King Jr. Day, and the Fourth of July. Maybe if you give it a cute name like the French do, you'll feel more willing to take a leap over that bridge and allow yourself the rest you deserve.

Changing your mentality from living to work to working to live may take time—it did for me—but it's a worthwhile ethos to consider. Your job is not who you are, but rather something you do. Sure, it's ideal if you enjoy it. Maybe it brings you happiness and fulfillment. But it *is* work, and its ultimate purpose is to pay for your day-to-day life and, certainly, your vacations. In my experience, the "just being" moments will ultimately bring more joy, happiness, and purpose than any nine-to-five job ever could.

MADAME'S PACKING LIST

Whether hitting the beach for a couple of days or the mountains for a whole month, don't forget to pack these essentials—even if the essentials are, say, special linens or particular serving trays that bring you joy. You do you, like I do me!

- **EARPLUGS OR HEADPHONES** for when you want to tune out (or in).

- **MAGAZINES OR BOOKS** for catching up on culture or being swept away in a story.

- **A SCENTED CANDLE** for adding ambience or a sense of familiarity to an unknown space.

- **SLIPPERS** for keeping the feet warm and cozy.

- **YOUR FAVORITE COFFEE OR TEA** to maintain your morning or afternoon rituals (especially if you're particular about taste).

- **EMPTY SPACE IN YOUR LUGGAGE OR EXTRA TOTE BAGS** for bringing home unexpected treasures.

- **A WATER BOTTLE OR TRAVEL MUG WITH A LID** to stay hydrated on trains, trails, and other adventures.

- **LINENS** for spontaneous picnics or to elevate any table in a vacay rental.

- **A SMALL OR MEDIUM SILVER TRAY** to create a solid, beautiful space on which to set drinks and food when out in nature.

Opposite
Château de Villiers–le–Mahieu is an all–inclusive weekend spot close to Paris with a country–home vibe.

WEEKEND GETAWAYS CLOSE TO PARIS

I have fully become a lady who weekends, constantly in search of short getaways. And while I enjoy exploring new places, I am also happy to return to places I've been before, to enjoy "holy days" alone or with friends or family. Here are a few of my favorite spots close to Paris to *faire le pont*.

MAISON CERONNE. Le Perche has become a popular weekend getaway region for Parisians. It's only about two to three hours from Paris by car or one and a half hours by train. (Though, it's best to have wheels in the region.) I'll admit to a moment of selfishness: At first, I didn't want to share this private home turned hotel with anyone, but joy is meant to be shared. This *maison* is particularly interesting for design lovers, as it is decorated with a superchic collection of furniture and art from periods spanning the 1950s to the '80s. There's also a heated indoor as well as an outdoor pool, a sauna, a hammam (steam room), a cinema, a karaoke room, a gym, a Japanese arcade, restaurants, lots of places to lounge, bikes for exploring, and more. It feels like a cozy, fun, and elegant escape all at the same time.

DOMAINE DE COURANCES. Built in the seventeenth century and still occupied by a family who live and visit year-round, this private property about an hour south of Paris by car is ideal for one or two nights in the countryside. I went for a cozy girls' weekend one fall, and we were tempted to stay in our little house drinking around the fire for weeks. I daresay they also have one of the most spectacular gardens in France, with statues, pavilions, and water fountains. *Courances* means "currents" or "streams" in English, and indeed, there are more than fourteen different springs on the property, plus a Japanese garden.

LE BARN. This is one of those spots that kept popping up in my Instagram feed, practically begging me to spend three days there for a mini writer's retreat—though, when I did, it was hard to get much done. I wanted to relax instead and watch all the chic Parisians who come for the day to dine at the property's popular farm-to-table restaurant. Le Barn is about an hour and fifteen minutes from Paris by car, in the Forêt de Rambouillet, one of France's national forests, so I understand the appeal of hopping in the car and popping down to the country for the afternoon. Kids and dogs can run free on the lawns, and there are even horses to ride. I loved simply sitting by the lake and taking in all that fresh country air.

LES MAISONS DE CAMPAGNE, CHÂTEAU DE VILLIERS-LE-MAHIEU. This getaway will forever be known as the one where I tried to teach my son, Baz (whom I brought with me solo), how to row a boat—that is, until I lost an oar and realized I didn't know *how* to row a boat. Thankfully, the castle-like property, which is only about an hour and twenty-three minutes from Paris by car, also has bikes for exploring, tennis courts and playgrounds for exercise, indoor and outdoor pools for swimming and splashing, and even an outdoor movie screen for cinema soirées—so, we remained in good spirits. It's also an all-inclusive stay—with the cost of meals, lodging, and activities covered in the price—so it was nice not to have to think about the bill once we arrived.

LES TILLEULS. I knew the original owners of this blink-and-you'll-miss-it house full of amazing antiques. Located almost two hours and forty-five minutes from Paris by car in the popular seaside town of Étretat (made famous by the impressionists), it has since changed hands, but the young woman who now runs it has maintained its cozy spirit and look, while adding a dose of hipsterism courtesy of yoga retreats and chef pop-ups. From the grounds, it's an easy walk to the *falaises* (giant cliffs) and, if you're feeling adventurous, a wonderful hike a bit farther along to the lighthouse. There's also a lovely sculpture garden worth visiting. Oh, and bring beach shoes. This one is rocky and not for bare feet!

DOMAINE DE PRIMARD. Technically, this incredible *domaine* (estate) is in the town of Guainville, about an hour's train ride from Paris, or an hour and a half by car. The closest attraction, about thirty minutes away from the *domaine* by car, is Monet's home in Giverny—if that's on your agenda, this is a great place to stay nearby. That being said, this lovely property is worth a visit in its own right, and not least because it was once the private estate of French actress Catherine Deneuve. Her former home now features three different buildings, each of which provides varying views and vibes. (Some rooms have private gardens, some look out on a lake, while rooms in the main house get to peek out on the manicured gardens and the ducks and geese roaming them.) There's also a Japanese spa with treatments using Susanne Kaufmann products—get the facial—and a restaurant with fresh cuisine featuring ingredients from their garden.

ON QUALITY

SEEK OUT THE
BEST INGREDIENTS

Opposite

The marché on Boulevard Richard–Lenoir is one of my favorite markets to shop for fruits and vegetables.

Good food is the foundation of genuine happiness.

—Auguste Escoffier, French chef, restaurateur, and author of Le Guide Culinaire

A BREAD APART

A baguette is a baguette, no? That's a *hard* no—which I learned when traveling with a group of friends to Giverny, a charming little town forty-five minutes from Paris and made famous by the painter Claude Monet.

It was a crisp September morning, and I volunteered to get groceries, dragging the only other American in the group with me. We wandered around the *marché* in the larger neighboring town of Vernon for the meat and produce and then decided to stop at the big grocery store on the edge of the town for a few extras. While grabbing canned items, condiments, and unnecessary toys for our kids, we realized that we had forgotten to get baguettes at the *marché* in town. *No big deal,* I thought. *The nearby supermarket has everything.* I snagged four and tossed them into our cart.

When we returned to the rental, my very French Lyonnais friend David and the other equally traditionalist David from Provence regarded the bread with expressions of suspicion bordering on disgust.

"What is this?" David Number One asked.

I thought it was a trick question and responded with a smirk and a giggle. "It's a baguette! What do you mean, 'What is this?'"

The other David asked, "Where did you get this?"

I was immediately confused and responded with a hint of sarcasm, "The store!" What did he think, that I picked it up in a field?

David Number Two: "What store?"

Me: "Why does it matter? A store!"

David Number One gave David Number Two a knowing look and said, "This isn't from a *boulangerie*." Then he tore off a piece of the bread, smooshed it, smelled it, inspected it, and then declared his assumption correct: *C'est du pain industriel!* he said, referring to commercially produced bread. "It's not a *baguette*."

I laughed uncomfortably, shocked to discover that he was serious. I realized then that I had committed a faux pas. I had purchased factory-produced bread and was trying to pass it off as a baguette.

That's right. All baguettes are not created equal. A mass-produced baguette, like the ones I'd gotten at the superstore, doesn't taste the same as a *boulangerie* baguette because it isn't made the same way. (Later, I learned it doesn't sound, smell, or look the same, either. See "How to Spot a Bona Fide Baguette," page 76, for more on that.)

One of the Davids jokingly (I think) declared, "That's the last time we send the Americans to buy the baguettes."

It was a pretty hilarious scene, but also a cautionary tale I have not forgotten. In France, *where* you buy the food you consume matters as much as, if not more than, the food itself. Food is necessary to survive, sure, but its origin is a vital source of joy.

See, the French love hunting and gathering for their ingredients—what they call *les bons produits* (the good products). Now that I live in France, I find myself answering questions or engaging in conversations about the food I buy and consume way more than I do when back in the States. People in France want to know *where* you bought something. For example, did you get the charcuterie from the *boucherie,* the Italian *épicerie,* or the *supermarché*? Did you buy your cheese from the *marché* or the *fromagerie*?

In France, French cuisine is discussed, dissected, praised, and even protected. UNESCO recognized and inscribed French gastronomy on its "Representative List of the Intangible Cultural Heritage of Humanity," in 2010. (Part of this designation includes *l'art de la table,* which we'll get into more in Lesson Three.)

After my first visit to Paris, I fell in love with all things French, including the food. When I lived in New York City, I frequented French restaurants like Bar Tabac in Cobble Hill and Le Bilboquet on the Upper East Side. My regular order? Steak frites, a fricassée salad, and a side of escargots.

Even though protecting my waistline now limits my intake of croissants and pain au chocolat, it's really hard to walk past a *boulangerie* in Paris and not be lured in. You can smell the layers of buttery pastries from the street and imagine every single, flaky bite. My stomach rumbles at the mere thought of classic bistro cuisine like boeuf bourguignon, onion soup, and confit de canard.

I could prattle on about French food forever—and I'm not the only one. But I have come to understand that the food is good because the ingredients are thoughtfully chosen.

Back to the baguette. Generally, it makes an appearance at every meal on nearly every dining table in France. If I invite friends for dinner, someone will ask if they should bring a baguette. And when you sit down to eat, someone will inevitably ask where the baguette is and which bakery it came from.

But a baguette is not necessarily fancy. Far from it, in fact. In France, it's rarely buttered, as it is used mostly to scrape up the sauce on a plate. It's also customary to rip it, rather than slice it, and French diners also tend to leave the untouched pieces right on the table.

The French value the baguette so much that laws are in place to restrict when *boulangeries* can open and close, so that the French always have access to a proper baguette.

What's more, every year in Paris, a baguette competition is held—the Grand Prix de la Baguette de Tradition Française de la Ville de Paris. The winning *boulangerie* is awarded major bragging rights, a financial prize, and an exclusive contract to provide baguettes to the president of France for a year. To qualify for this competition, the baguette must meet strict rules for size, weight, salt content, aroma, appearance, crispiness, and, of course, taste. There are also rules as to what can be called a *baguette tradition*. It must be made from only four ingredients: wheat flour, water, yeast, and salt.

Further cementing its status as the bread of choice in France is this little historical tidbit: While Americans were hoarding toilet paper during the 2020 pandemic, the French were forming epic lines and hoarding baguettes—this despite the fact that a baguette's average shelf life is about four to six hours. Evidently, real baguettes are essential.

Tip

The French don't really bother with bread-and-butter plates, unless you're at a fancy restaurant. Instead, they serve the bread in baskets for enjoying directly on the table. So feel free to skip this extra plate at home.

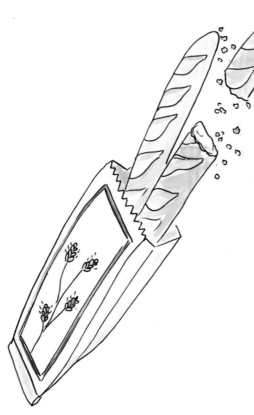

HOW TO SPOT A BONA FIDE BAGUETTE

Tip

*The end of the baguette is called
the* croûton. *People fight over it
at the dinner table or will tear it
off and eat it while walking home
from the* boulangerie.

How can you tell if your baguette is worthy?

◊ The exterior has color because there is no
bleach in the flour.

◊ It doesn't shatter when you squeeze it (but
crumbs are okay once you tear it).

◊ It has a nice, golden *croûte,* or "crust," that
makes a satisfyingly subtle crackling sound.

◊ When you break it apart, there are many
holes inside—the mark of natural yeast,
which gives the bread a more complex flavor.

◊ The yeast holes are about the same size.

◊ The inside of the baguette is stretchy and
elastic.

◊ The inside is soft and fluffy, not chewy.

◊ It was made with absolutely no additives or
preservatives.

HUNTING AND GATHERING

Let's be honest, supermarkets and grocery stores—known as *hypermarchés* in French—are convenient no matter where you live. The bigger they are, the more choices you'll find. Offering one-stop shopping, these big-box superstores first hit the scene in France in the 1950s, as part of urbanism and regional planning, and then really had a boom and expansion in the 1980s and '90s. Such stores are ideal for people living in rural areas who might not find what they want at the small shops in town. But modernization, while necessary, comes with a price. In France, that price has been the death of small shops and city centers and the encroachment of ugliness (or, to put it kindlier, a lack of a certain *je ne sais quoi,* depending on whom you ask).

In 2019, the French newspaper *L'Obs* titled an article "Faut-il fermer les hypermarchés, accusés d'avoir tué le petit commerce?" ("Should We Close the Supermarkets Accused of Having Killed Small Business?"). It questioned the intentions of heads at two major retail chains, blaming them for turning beautiful country landscapes into ugly industrial zones with their warehouse-size stores. But even with said accusations and consequences, we consumers still shop there.

My standard food shopping experience at a big-box store, whether here in France or in the United States, goes something like this: I push a big metal cart down neon-lighted aisles while choosing among many brands of the same product (or, in New York City, I squeeze down narrow aisles in a corner deli, stacking as many items as I can hold in my own two arms), then go through the checkout rarely exchanging more than a "Thanks" or a "Have a nice day" with the store employee. In other words, it's impersonal and uninspiring. The goal is to get in and get out.

Now, imagine if you will, my trip to the smaller *marché,* in Paris. (And let's say it's a warm, sunny day, because imagination means we can choose our own adventure.) I have a wicker (not a plastic) basket swinging over my arm as I walk down the sidewalks looking at piles of fresh fruits and vegetables, tables of stacked cheeses, recently caught fish on ice, and roasted chickens turning on spits. When I approach a colorful stack of produce, the vendor offers me a taste of a brightly colored fruit.

Opposite

The farmers' market can be a place of inspiration as you walk through and find fresh ingredients for what you want to prepare.

In France, *where* you buy the food you consume matters as much as, if not more than, the food itself. Food is necessary to survive, sure, but its origin is a vital source of joy.

I contemplate the morsel of fruit in his outstretched hand (forgetting to think about germs), and he makes a joke I don't totally get, but I laugh anyway. We strike up a conversation. I explain to him what I want to cook that evening, and he helps me choose ripe fruit for that night's meal and some other fruit that will age in a few days. I pay for my purchases, wander past a street musician, and then head to the fish stand to discuss how many oysters are ideal for an *apéro*.

Some days, I might even pop into my local *fromagerie* (cheesemonger) to ask for his help making a cheese tray for a party of five. He tells me what's in season and helps me choose a variety of hard and soft cheeses, letting me taste a few. (I know. I, too, did not know that cheese was seasonal!)

Finally, I stop at my *caviste,* or "wine merchant," to see how his new baby is doing and ask for a dry white wine with zero sulfates to pair with the oysters.

The second experience might take longer than popping into a supermarket, but it is incomparable and feels vastly different from being in a supermarket. I don't do this every single day, but I do it often, because I love how the smaller stores connect me to my community and to French culture. I love talking to all the vendors at these various stops. They remember me, and I feel a sense of belonging. I trust that they want me to enjoy what I buy from them. Not only are these people specialists, but they're also interested in and passionate about sharing their knowledge. Most days, I eat up their tips like an eager student wanting to learn more, more, more, and I leave feeling confident and a moment of joie de vivre while getting my groceries.

So, you see, the two shopping experiences are just not the same.

Hypermarchés are necessary, but France realizes they are affecting small businesses and causing a deterioration of the essence of small-town life. In 2018, France passed the ELAN law, which focuses mostly on housing, but also on the "revitalization of the commercial fabric of the city center." I appreciate that the French government is finding ways to protect and preserve small specialty shops and our need to hunt and gather as a community.

These days, consumers want to know where their goods come from and are interested in supporting small businesses they know and trust. Neighbors of mine—both well-known French journalists—told me they believe there is a collective nostalgia for rural life taking place right now. In rural communities, markets and cafés provide opportunities to speak with people and make connections.

I have noticed this change taking place. Even my local Monoprix (a popular chain *hypermarché*) installed a *poissonnerie* and *fromagerie* within the store, where you can speak directly to someone who will help you choose what to buy and will answer any questions. When I am in Provence, I've noticed that most of the superstores there have their own specialists, in an attempt to mimic the expertise and shopping experience one would find at smaller specialty shops.

We humans need connection for our mental and physical health. We need to connect with other people literally to survive. Hear that? You can actually improve your health by, once a week (or even once a month, if once a week seems aggressive), popping into a smaller specialty shop to get your groceries. When I lived in New York during my twenties and early thirties, the Fresh Direct delivery dude was the only human connection I had with regard to what I bought to nourish my body. I'd sit in front of my computer, click around to choose what I wanted, and the next day, a rather grumpy guy would haul my stuff up four flights of stairs. (Not to say that all delivery guys are grumpy, but most people didn't smile after bringing three to four large boxes up that wonky walk-up.) There wasn't a lot of chitchat going on. The delivery guy would be sweaty and exhausted, and just wanted me to sign for my groceries. This wasn't the kind of human connection that would improve my health and happiness—or his, for that matter.

In his book *Social,* Matthew Lieberman claims that interpersonal connection is a core human need right up there with food and water. According to *Psychology Today,* without such connection, we increase our chances of depression and various illnesses. (I will spare you the grim stats of which illnesses.)

If we approach shopping for food as a communal activity, as the French do, not only will the connections we make strengthen our sense of empathy and community, no matter where we live, but our sense of joy will increase, and we will learn from the people we encounter in the process.

Patronizing small businesses is also a great way to discover and connect with a specific city or region. The locals are usually proud to talk in depth (sometimes too much) about what makes their products unique to the region. Visit the markets in the South of France to buy herbs de Provence, lavender-infused honey, or nougat. Go to a *fromagerie* in the Savoie to try their Beaufort cheese; or to one in Bourgogne for their Époisses (which smells like old socks, but tastes divine— trust me). Buy *canelés* (pastries flavored with rum) from a pâtisserie in Bordeaux, *kouign-amann* or *far breton* (both sweet cakes) from Bretagne, or visit a butcher in Corsica and try some of the *cochon noir* (black pork).

And while we're diving into the psychology of *why* you should take a break from the big supermarket once in a while, let's look at the science behind "emotional contagion." In an article for *Positive Psychology,* Dr. Jeffrey Gaines, a clinical psychologist specializing in neuropsychology, wrote that, yes, emotions are contagious. When we are around people who are happy, we feel happy. When we are around people who are angry, we feel angry. What if we interact with someone who is knowledgeable and passionate about what they do, who gets pleasure from what they do? That's right, friends. We'll feel that, too.

WHAT'S SO SPECIAL ABOUT SPECIALTY STORES?

Don't let the need for efficiency (aka one-stop shops or online grocery shopping) deprive you of necessary human connection, moments of joy, or the chance to learn about the food you consume and how it makes you feel. Visit the *marché* (farmers' market) on market days and support your local specialty stores. Get to know your community connoisseurs. Instead of bulk shopping, try buying food as needed. Linger and savor rather than click, check out, and repeat.

Paris has no shortage of specialty stores, and over time, I have learned what to look for when I pop in. The following is a list of a few of my favorites in Paris and some advice on distinguishing one from the other.

LE CROTTIN
PYRÉNÉEN
Fermier
Aydius - Pyrénées -
Atlantique
Ferme Bourguinat
Lait cru
25% MG
3,80€/u

CHÈVRE FRAIS
fermier
Joursac - Cantal
GAEC Reuss
Lait cru
4,75€/p

LA COURONNE
D'AYDIUS
fermier
Aydius - Pyrénées
Ferme de Bourguinat
Lait cru cedar
6,50€/u

LOCH

Froidevaux
Brebis
Lait cru

FROMAGERIE OR CRÈMERIE— CHEESEMONGER

A pungent pit stop when you are making the rounds, a *fromagerie* or *crèmerie* will have all the cheeses you never knew existed and then some. (Be prepared for a smack to the nostrils when you walk in.) Find out what's in season (some cheeses have seasons because of the weather, what the animals are eating, et cetera), and buy locally made products. And don't be shy! Ask for recommendations.

FROMAGERIE LAURENT DUBOIS
97–99 rue Saint-Antoine, 75004

LA FROMAGERIE GONCOURT
1 rue Abel Rabaud, 75011

TAKA & VERMO
61 bis rue du Faubourg Saint-Denis, 75010

POISSONNERIE— FISHMONGER

Guard thy nostrils again; this is another stinky shop—but the good stinky, not the day-old kind. Just like at the butcher's, here they'll ask you how much you want in weight or quantity and will be happy to help you choose a filet or a bag of shellfish based on your preparation method and budget. Come Christmastime, this is where to come for oysters, which the French slurp like they do wine. This is a shop Parisians choose based on proximity to their kitchen, for obvious reasons.

LE HOMARD PARISIEN
21 rue Rambuteau, 75004

SOGUISA
62-72 rue Montorgueil, 75002

Above
La Fromagerie Goncourt.

Opposite
Most *fromageries* let you sample some cheeses before you make your selection based on your preference, what is in season, and their suggestions.

BOULANGERIE—JUST BREAD . . . MOSTLY

Welcome to carb heaven. This is where you come for bread—be it a *baguette tradition*, a *pain de campagne* (country-style bread), or any number of loaves, be they seeded or *nature* (plain), sliced or *complet* (whole), as well as *viennoiserie* pastries such as croissants, pain au chocolat, brioche, or *chaussons aux pommes* (apple turnovers).

DU PAIN ET DES IDÉES
34 rue Yves Toudic, 75010

URBAN BAKERY
67 rue du Faubourg du Temple, 75010

THE FRENCH BASTARDS
61 rue Oberkampf, 75011

Tip

Because this is France, and they make their own rules, sometimes you'll find a boulangerie-pâtisserie, which makes both bread and pastries.

Opposite

Desserts from Fou de Pâtisserie, made by the best pastry chefs in Paris.

BOUCHERIE—BUTCHER

Prepare to see and smell lots of raw meat. Beef, veal, pork—you name it, they'll chop it and weigh it. They usually ask how much you want (in weight) or how many people you're serving. Personally, I always round up, because I like to have leftovers. A butcher loves to share tips on how to cook your meat, so this is another chance to charm and be charmed. These guys (and some girls) are full of information and, generally, Parisians favor the butchers located in their neighborhood.

LA BOUCHERIE HAYÉE PATRICK
Marché Beauvau, place d'Aligre, 75012

LA BOUCHERIE ROGER MONTORGUEIL
62 rue Montorgueil, 75002

PÂTISSERIE—JUST DESSERTS . . . MOSTLY

Generally, these stores sell just desserts—I'm talkin' pastry cream, Chantilly, praline, meringue, chocolate—all the sweetness squeezed into the likes of tartes, éclairs, or chou. In Paris, you've got your neighborhood pâtisseries and then you've got award-winning pâtisseries worth crossing town for. Either way, *Courage!*—good luck in choosing.

FOU DE PÂTISSERIE
45 rue Montorgueil, 75002

LA PÂTISSERIE CYRIL LIGNAC
24 rue Paul Bert, 75011

SÉBASTIEN GAUDARD
22 rue des Martyrs, 75009

STOHRER PARIS
51 rue Montorgueil, 75002

ÉPICERIE AND LEGUMES— GREENGROCER OR LOCAL SHOP

There's one more very important specialty shop I call the extras-you-didn't-know-you-needed shop. Here, you'll find artisanal mustard, and jam made by an independent seller, and a selection of homemade pastas and premade soups, and salted cashews sprinkled with spices. Think of it as an upscale supermarket. Many *épiceries* also sell a selection of specialty produce you may not find in grocery stores, such as *topinambour* (Jerusalem artichoke) or *romanesco* (a type of cauliflower). They're great for those days when you didn't wake up in time to make it to the *marché* or you want a special tapenade to take along to an *apéro*.

CŒUR ÉPICERIE SAINE
18 rue du Général Guilhem, 75011

IZRAËL
30 rue François Miron, 75004

LA GRANDE ÉPICERIE
38 rue de Sèvres, 75007

TERROIRS D'AVENIR
84 rue Jean-Pierre Timbaud, 75011

CAVE À VINS—WINE CELLAR

True story: Many wine stores were considered "essential" during the Covid-19 pandemic and remained open—despite the fact that many supermarkets offer a huge selection of wine. But we're shopping small, right? Remember, in France, the emphasis is on the region, not the grape. And while the *caviste* (wine merchant) won't necessarily turn down your money if you say you want a pinot noir, it's definitely helpful to know that might mean you'd like a red from Burgundy, where those grapes are heavily grown. Also, some *caves* have a small bar where you can sit and taste open bottles before you buy.

LA CAVE DE BELLEVILLE
51 rue de Belleville, 75019

LA CAVE DU DARON
140 avenue Parmentier, 75011

LE VERRE VOLÉ
54 rue de la Folie Méricourt, 75011

Above
La Cave du Daron, run by a man named Frederique, is a friendly neighborhood wine cellar in the 11th arrondissement.

Opposite
Cœur Épicerie Saine near Square Gardette is a nice stop to find healthy pantry items and produce on a charming little street.

FAIT MAISON

When my daughter was eight, she decided to
create her own lemonade stand. She insisted
we go to the *marché,* not the supermarket, to get
lemons and a few other fruits. Then she happily
chopped and squeezed everything to whip up
her concoction. When everything was ready,
and because she is growing up in the digital age,
she asked me to make a video. In the video, she
introduces herself, gives a speech about how
to make a lemonade stand, takes a sip of the
lemonade she's made, holds up a finger, and
says, "Yummm! Made house!" I just about died
laughing at her literal translation of the French
phrase *fait maison,* which means "homemade." But
I was also pretty impressed that such a description
was so important to her. She had clearly picked
it up from our lives in Paris—something's being
homemade is an important selling point at
restaurants or wherever you order food.

In 2014, France passed a law stating that
restaurants and catering services needed to
publicly advertise if their dishes were *fait maison.*
In an effort to help uphold and maintain French
culinary standards, especially after the UNESCO
anointing, the goal was to provide transparency
and to educate consumers about whether their
food was made from fresh, quality, seasonal
ingredients and was not factory-produced,
prepackaged, frozen and reheated. The official
government site states that "homemade" is
synonymous with the title *maître-restaurateur*
because "French and seasonal products, local
supplies, quality of the setting and service . . . are
two systems that are complementary, they are part
of a dynamic of quality and transparency . . ." For
France, no chef or restaurant can be considered
great unless the quality of the food is good. And
in this case, many "industrial" and prepackaged
foods are not as interesting, *joie*-inducing, or
worthy of protection.

As I noted at the beginning of this chapter,
when the ingredients are good, the food is sure
to be good. I am impressed that a law was created
to highlight and regulate this. The experience of
eating at a brasserie that defrosts the food can't
possibly be the same as eating at a brasserie where
the chef and his team go to the *marché* to source
les bons produits and prepare the meals fresh.

STUDY, SIP, AND SAVOR

My dear friend Sassoum, who introduced me to my husband, was coming to our place for dinner to celebrate our engagement, so I popped over to our local supermarket to grab some wine. Looking at a wall of amber and green bottles, I scanned the prices and pretty labels as I always do and quickly settled on a five-euro bottle of Côtes du Rhône. My very French guest arrived, took a sip, and immediately launched an inquisition into why I had chosen that particular bottle. I knew absolutely nothing about it other than that I had picked it out of a grocery store lineup an hour before she arrived and that the price had been right. She was shocked to hear me excitedly brag about catching a deal at a supermarket for the wine without having obtained information about what we were drinking. It was the baguette debacle all over again. (What can I say? I'm a slow learner.)

As with bread, the French love to talk about wine. During my time in France, I have endured epic dinner conversations observing the (sometimes fanatical) pleasure my French companions derive from the subject. For the French, this education starts from an early age (about sixteen or seventeen) with a glass of wine once in a while at the family dining table or a glass of champagne for New Year's Eve. It makes sense that whether you are listening to adults discuss wine or having a taste of it yourself as a teenager, you might slowly develop a deeper appreciation for the grape—unlike my own education, which cultivated wine as a means to an end: getting drunk.

There are a plethora of vineyards and champagne houses in France where you can learn about the history of winemaking, grapes, and *terroir* (yes, even the soil is particularly interesting to the French). Doing so aids in fostering appreciation of and pleasure in drinking wine.

When I moved here, and was excitedly snatching up bottles I had chosen by price, I didn't make any attempt to learn about wine by visiting houses or going to tastings. My choices are different now because of my curiosity to know what I am consuming. Learning about wine has led to meeting friends in Sancerre; to visiting the Domaine de La Perrière winery, which is built inside a grotto; and to planning family outings to the superchic Château l'Hospitalet, owned by wine legend Gérard Bertrand (whose bottles you can often find in American stores). And then there was the mini girls' trip to Beaune to visit the D'Ardhuy family winery (see "A Chat with a Woman Winemaker," page 102), where I finally learned what makes a *cru* versus a *grand cru*. (Spoiler: It's the *terroir!*)

If you want to know more about wine:

1. Be curious and visit wineries.

2. Don't base your decision solely on price.

3. Visit your local *caviste* and ask their opinion.

4. Admit you don't know much, but share what you do know.

5. Savor that glass and focus on what you're tasting.

Tip

There are approximately 360 champagne houses and 27,000 wineries in France, many of which you can visit.

Opposite

The dramatic grand entry to the Domaine d'Ardhuy on the edge of Beaune in Burgundy.

A CASE FOR COUPES

There's a myth that the champagne coupe was molded after Marie Antoinette's left breast—a notion I absolutely love. In fact, I often hold my glass to my chest, pretending it's true. But alas, it's false folklore. The champagne coupe predates the French queen and is said to have been invented in England circa 1663.

The first depiction of the coupe appears in a painting by Jean-François de Troy (1679–1752) called *Le Déjeuner d'huîtres* (1735), which hung in Louis XV's private dining room. In it, revelers are seen enjoying oysters, popping bottles of bubbly, and drinking it from coupes. Some things haven't changed, like the perfect pairing of champagne with oysters, but back then, they downed each glass like a shot, hence the coupe's shallow bowl.

The coupe was the champagne glass of choice from the 1700s in France through the 1970s and from the 1920s in the United States until it was dethroned by the flute, which hit the scene thirty years later. Champagne enthusiasts prefer the flute because it supposedly maintains the bubbles longer, thanks to its tubular shape. I love to look at bubbles as much as the next person, but I enjoy drinking them even more—from a coupe. Why? Call me a hopeless romantic, but I appreciate the coupe's femininity and sinewy beauty. It takes me back to some of my favorite eras, like the Roaring Twenties, the days of Hollywood glamour of the 1940s and '50s, and even the *Mad Men* era a decade after that. I highly encourage you to pour yourself a cocktail, a glass of champagne, or even juice in an antique coupe and enjoy that glam feeling.

Oh, and here's a little style tip: The coupes don't need to be uniform. In fact, it's fun to mix and match coupes. This way, you won't need a full set. I love having a cabinet full of different beauties. My guests almost never mix up their glasses, and they enjoy a new beveled or etched wonder every time they come over to share a drink with me.

Opposite
I have a 1950s black sideboard with a growing collection of mix-and-match glassware so guests never mix up their coupes.

VIVE LE TERROIR— OR, WHY WE SHOULD CARE ABOUT DIRT

Opposite
The vines in Beaune make for a lovely drive through Burgundy.

It took me quite some time to really understand why the French love talking about *le terroir,* which translates literally to "the soil." Why in the world would soil be so important or conversation-worthy to anyone who wasn't a farmer? It's dirt! The idea of *terroir* seemed obtuse and strange to me until I dug a little deeper. According to Steven Erlanger of *The New York Times,* "The importance of *terroir* to the French psyche and self-image is difficult to overestimate, because it is a concept almost untranslatable, combining soil, weather, region and notions of authenticity, of genuineness and particularity—of roots, and home—in contrast to globalized products designed to taste the same everywhere."

Let's unpack that a bit more:

IRREPLACEABLE: *Terroir* is dirt from a specific place that cannot be replicated in another place. Everything, from the location and climate of this specific *terroir,* contributes to its uniqueness. Tanisha Townsend, fellow expat, wine educator, and the girl behind Girl Meets Glass wine tours and the podcast *Wine School Dropout,* says, "It's not just soil, but it is land, and there are various land types. Is the land hilly? Is it flat? Then the climate affects that land in different ways, creating distinct flavor profiles. You can have the same grape growing in a few different places, and it will not taste the same."

FLAVOR: The conditions of the *terroir* contribute to the way food (vegetables and wheat eaten by animals) and wine (grapes grown in dirt versus sand versus rock) tastes the way they do. I used to go around declaring that I hated chardonnay, until Tanisha informed me that one of my favorite wines from the region of Chablis was, in fact, made from Chardonnay grapes!

CONTROLLABLE: L'Appellation d'Origine Protégée/Contrôlée (AOP/AOC) protects and authenticates regions of France and the products from those regions. (This explains why you can't buy a sparkling wine from Provence and call it "champagne"; champagne hails only from the region of Champagne.) Meanwhile, the Institut National de l'Origine et de la Qualité, a branch of the French Ministry of Agriculture, ensures the quality of food and beverages.

A CHAT WITH
A WOMAN
WINEMAKER

MIREILLE D'ARDHUY-SANTIARD
Co-owner of Domaine d'Ardhuy

One of the first wedding tables I styled was for fellow expat and photographer Joann Pai's marriage to French art director Benoît Santiard. It was at their nuptials that I first met Benoît's mother, Mireille d'Ardhuy-Santiard, who, along with her six sisters, inherited their father's vineyard. There aren't many female winemakers out there, and I was so impressed that, four years later, I rounded up a few of my wine-loving friends to visit the vineyards of Beaune, where Mireille and her family grow grapes. Ever the grape-growing host, Mireille was gracious enough to educate me further.

Q: What do you love most about making wine?

A: It's a different product every year, and it's always a challenge. But I love the idea of participating in the creation of a work that provides pleasure to people.

Opposite
On a girl's trip to Beaune we stopped for a tasting at the Domaine d'Ardhuy where Mireille welcomed us and shared her best wines.

Q: Is there a part of the annual process you most look forward to, year after year?

A: Tasting every day during the vinification and the aging in the barrel. Also, the tasting with the team after the wine is ready to be bottled and the slight stress waiting for the comments of experts and customers.

Q: What is unique about your wines and the *terroir* where they're grown?

A: We work with a spirit of biodynamic pruning, in order to get lower crops for quality and concentration. The wine produced in each plot must show the characteristics of the *terroir* where it comes from, so we use a great number of small vats, which allows us to [vinify] separately each single part of the plot according to the maturity and health stage. We are careful not to have too many new oak barrels, in order to keep the distinct taste and aromas of each vineyard.

Q: Other than your own *terroir,* what is your second-favorite wine-growing region in France—and the world?

A: The Rhône Valley, since we also have a family *domaine* there—Domaine la Cabotte, near Orange, France—created by my father and run by my sister Marie-Pierre her husband, Éric, and son, Étienne. I like the region's diversity and, most especially, those who are showing more finesse and elegance rather than power.

Q: What sort of advice can you share with those who are timid or less knowledgeable about wine?

A: There is no recipe. The best wine is the wine the taster prefers according to his individual desires—whether it's white, rosé, or red; sweet or dry; cheap or expensive. The knowledge of wines comes after many tastings and discussions with people who are amateurs or experts.

Q: What makes these flavors appear in the wine? For example, wine tastes drier or more mineral because . . .

A: First of all, it's the *terroir* and the composition of the soil (limestone, clay, sandstone, sand, or slate); then it's the climate (sunny, windy, rainy); and then you have the grape variety (chardonnay, pinot, muscat, viognier, grenache, or syrah).

Q: Can you recommend some wine from your region?

A: Here in Burgundy, we try to think about wine in the context of how we consume it and what we enjoy it with. For example, for an *apéritif,* try something dry, young, and vibrant, like a white Hautes Côtes de Beaune. For grilled fish, I would suggest a white Savigny-lès-Beaune or a Pernand-Vergelesses. With grilled meat, I would suggest a red Bourgogne, such as Ladoix or Savigny-lés-Beaune.

A CHAT WITH A WINE EDUCATOR

TANISHA TOWNSEND

Founder of Girl Meets Glass and host of the
Wine School Dropout podcast

When I hosted an *apéro* for my friend Monique, who was coming to town to share her vintage bottle of Château Margaux, she insisted that the person to open, decant, and teach us all about this wine should be none other than Tanisha Townsend. A girl from the South Side of Chicago, Tanisha has been living in Paris for several years working as a wine educator and wine tour guide. She is often a coveted judge for various competitions across Europe and was recently inducted into the wine brotherhood of Échansonnerie des Papes. Tanisha always breaks things down in a way I can understand.

Above

Tanisha at Hôtel du Nord, a classic spot on the canal for a meal, café, or glass of wine.

Q: What do you love most about being a wine educator?

A: I love the people I interact with. There are the people I take on tours, the people I teach in classes, or people that I've stopped to chat with in a wine shop that didn't quite understand what they wanted to buy. I love helping people find something they will enjoy.

Q: What advice can you share for people who are timid or less knowledgeable about wine?

A: Don't automatically say you don't like something before trying it from various areas. For example, if you don't like merlot from California, then try one from Bordeaux, in France. Do you like pinot grigio from California? Try one from Italy as well. Try something that you think you might not like and then try it from a different place. Try, try, try!

Q: Where can we learn more about wine in a less intimidating way?

A: If you really want to get into wine and explore, you need to visit a wine shop. Why? At a wine shop, the owner and workers are trained and know their inventory. They will usually also have a scheduled tasting you can attend. Say you taste three wines there and you're like, *Oh, I hate all three of these*. Well, fantastic! Those are three wines you know you don't like, and you don't have to try those again.

Q: What descriptive words can we use to home in on what we like? For example, I tend to ask for something dry or minerally, sometimes fruity but not too fruity. Let's start with white wine.

A: Okay. Those you mentioned are great, but also *oaky, buttery*—and get specific with the fruit. Do you like tropical fruit, tree fruit, stone fruit? These tastes are very different profiles of wine. Maybe you like a little spice. I mean black pepper, nutmeg, and cinnamon. That kind of thing. Not spice like, *This wine is hot!* No, no, no! Not that kind of spice. Also, if there is a wine that you regularly drink, you can share that, too. It helps narrow things down a bit to help a wine shop know what to recommend that you will enjoy.

Q: And what about red?

A: With red, use *oak* as well, but also *meaty* or a *leathery* kind of smell and flavor. There are also tannins, which come from the use of oak barrels and the grape skins. Again, there will be the fruit, but darker fruits like plum, cherry, blackberry, and cassis. Also, vegetables like green pepper, as well as spice again.

Q: Why do these flavors appear in the wine?

A: Well, an oak flavor develops when the wine is aged in barrels. A mineral flavor comes from the soil. For example, if the *terroir* consists of limestone or chalky soil, then that flavor gets passed on to the vines and then to the grapes. If it is from soil that used to be underwater millions of years ago, well—this might creep you out—you have the carcasses of sea creatures in the soil. In that case, you will get a briny, saline kind of flavor to some

of the wines as well. Fruit flavors come from the sunlight and the rainfall and that kind of thing.

Q: So, if there is a fruit flavor, does that mean fruits are grown nearby?

A: Not necessarily. I was at a wine festival, and I was tasting cherries and strawberries. Why did it taste like cherries? Did you crush cherries into the wine? [She giggles.] I learned that it is just something that comes through the fermentation process of different flavors. So, it's nothing that can be specifically explained, but it's just certain grapes, which have certain flavors when they're grown properly. That part fascinates me!

Q: How can we truly savor a glass of wine?

A: To start, don't drink it right away. Let air come in contact with it. Swirl it. Sniff it. And then, when you put it in your mouth, hold it for a second, to feel where it is on your tongue. When you do tastings, after you hold it in your mouth, you kind of suck it—but if you're out at dinner, don't do that. You'll look crazy. But hold it in your mouth. Think about what kind of flavors you get. And then swallow it. See how long you can still taste it.

Q: There are different grapes and there are different regions. Which do we use to describe wine? By the grape or by the region or country?

A: France, Italy, and Spain describe wine on the label by region, because that's what's important to them. It has its own special something because of the *terroir*. For example, in France, you would say a Bordeaux. But everywhere else—like Australia, New Zealand, South Africa, America, Chile, Argentina—they focus on identifying wine by the grape. So, they might talk about wine as a pinot noir or a merlot.

HAPPY HOUR À LA FRANÇAISE

Apéro is one of my favorite rituals and a moment that brings so many French people *joie*. It's most similar to American happy hour when it comes to the timing, because it occurs in late afternoon or before dinner. However, it's not necessarily about getting two-for-one drinks and free olives or popcorn. It's more of a no-fuss, casual drinks-and-nibbles gathering—done either at a café or bistro that opens early or, more typically, at one's home.

I remember making the disastrous faux pas once of trying to prepare an elaborate spread for an *apéro*. I made several fancy dips with toasted pita bread, leek tartelettes, prosciutto-wrapped asparagus, endives with dollops of Boursin cheese, and bacon-wrapped dates. My French girlfriend Géraldine turned to me and said, "Ajiri, this is the *apéro* and not the meal, right?" *Oof!* That hurt!

It took me a while to learn that *apéro* is a moment of conviviality when one whets the appetite but doesn't spoil it. You can serve *kir,* which is white wine or champagne with a bit of crème de cassis; a coupe of champagne; or Lillet alongside a grazing board of charcuterie and crudités or, more simply, pretty bowls of nuts and chips . . . *et voilà!*

The *apéro* is an immensely pleasurable moment with friends that sometimes rolls into dinner—in which case, it's called an *apéro-dinatoire*. Indeed, there have been many times when we've gotten so caught up in the drinks and nibbles that we suddenly realized we were tipsy, starving, and couldn't eat another olive or chip. When we haven't already planned dinner, we might raid the kitchen cabinets to add heartier additions, like a salad or pasta. You can also plan to host an *apéro-dinatoire,* in which case you are fully prepared with more filling options. Whether *apéro* is a precursor to dinner or morphs into one, these simple, uncomplicated, and *joie*-infused moments of pure pleasure are to be savored with friends.

Tip

If someone invites you over for an apéro *around eight* P.M., *it most likely will turn into an* apéro-dinatoire. *I think we like to invite people over for an* apéro *even when we know it might transform into more than that because the casual unseated vibe is so welcoming and unintimidating. Who doesn't love standing around a kitchen island or on a terrace?*

APÉRO CHEAT SHEET

Apéro is a cherished way to gather that is no-fuss because it usually doesn't involve cooking. There are many ways to approach hosting your own *apéro*. Whether it is a spontaneous *apéro* or a planned *apéro* before dinner—at which point it becomes late and . . . oops! "We need to roll this into dinner," aka *apéro-dinatoire*—here are a few suggestions for choosing which one to host. I have included some food suggestions, but feel free to add what you want and rotate new ideas in and out. Whatever you decide, keep it easy and beautiful.

SIDEBOARD STOCK LIST

◊ Cutting boards

◊ Platters

◊ Serving plate or bowl with multiple compartments

◊ Little decorative bowls

◊ Utensils (little spoons, cheese knives, forks, and toothpicks)

INGREDIENTS

◊ Charcuterie

◊ Terrines, pâtés, *rillettes* (seasoned meat spread)

◊ Cheese (if you don't live in France—if you do live in France, the cheese is served before dessert only as part of an *apéro-dinatoire*)

◊ Nuts

◊ Fruits and vegetables

◊ Baguettes

◊ Chips, crackers, or any crunchy snack

◊ Olives

◊ Dips

◊ Flavored butters

◊ Salts

Opposite
Keep things simple and chic for a pre-dinner *apéro*.

1. THE DRINKS

◊ Planning: Low-level; visit your local *cave à vins* a few hours before

◊ Tools: A wineglass, champagne coupe, or flute of any height (the French are not as fussy about wineglasses as Americans are)

◊ Drink suggestions: Something light but on the sweeter side; kir (white wine with a drop or two of crème de cassis); a light, crisp white wine; champagne; or a Lillet on ice

2. THE LAST-MINUTE *APÉRO*

◊ Planning: Low-level; pull items from your pantry

◊ Tools: Decorative bowls or *apéro* servers with two to three compartments

◊ Food suggestions: Olives, peanuts, chips; crudités like carrots, cucumbers, and radishes; dips such as hummus or guacamole; salted butter; salt, if you go with radishes

3. THE PRE-DINNER *APÉRO*

◊ Planning: Mid-level; visit specialty shops and the market a few hours before

◊ Tools: Cutting board, platters, decorative bowls or *apéro* servers with two to three compartments

◊ Food suggestions: Charcuterie, smoked salmon, vegetables, dips such as hummus, blinis, *grostini,* chips

4. THE *APÉRO-DINATOIRE*

◊ Planning: Advance planning needed, with trips to the *marché* and specialty stores

◊ Tools: One to two cutting boards, tiny bowls, little spoons, additional serving utensils, platters and bowls

◊ Food suggestions: Oysters, charcuterie, patés, cheese, *confiture* (jam), nuts, vegetables, fruit, dips, and for more filling options: salads, light pasta, tartes or quiche, roasted vegetables

ON
GATHERING

BRING PEOPLE TOGETHER
WITH PURPOSE AND PRETTY THINGS

Opposite

My friend Vanessa often invites us to her country house outside of Paris for long, epic lunches. No meal is ever served on time and nothing is perfect, but no one cares because we have the best time gathering all together.

At the end of the day people won't remember what you said or did, they will remember how you made them feel.

—*Dr. Maya Angelou*

THE *JOIE* OF FELLOWSHIP

The importance of fellowship and gathering was instilled in me early as a Nigerian. The need to entertain with fancy table settings, many utensils, and intimidating etiquette rules, however, was not. When I was growing up in Austin, Texas, every Saturday (after garage sale shopping), we would get dressed up and meet with other Nigerian families through a group called African Christian Fellowship (ACF). (I would have preferred to camouflage myself into the couch and watch cartoons or run around the neighborhood with friends, but nope; I had no choice. I had to put on a semi-decent outfit and head off to the ACF.) The group was created as a way for Nigerian immigrant families to form a community and connect while also preserving their culture of origin with their American-raised children. We ate, we sang, we played, we talked, and we drank lots of sugary drinks. (It doesn't sound too bad, does it?) The adults loved coming together after a long week to spend time with their friends. If it was a kid's birthday, there would be cake and candy alongside the weekly aluminum foil–covered vats of fried rice, jollof rice, goat meat, and stew. If one of the adults had just graduated from university or a kid had graduated to middle school, there would be even more cake. We organized picnics so we could barbecue and conferences to connect with other chapters of ACF for more dancing, singing, and food. On Sundays after church, we sometimes met up with other friends (both Nigerian and non-Nigerian) for more music and food.

Essentially, Nigerians notoriously love gatherings, and from the time I started forming memories, they put truth to the words of the early twentieth-century textile designer William Morris, "Fellowship is life."

When I moved to New York in my twenties, after my undergrad years in Texas, I found another group that valued fellowship: Mexican girls who had grown up together in Juarez and El Paso. Mexican culture is very similar to Nigerian culture in that we both really love finding excuses to celebrate with one another in a big way. (Mexican weddings and Nigerian weddings are usually giant, full of extended family, and party crashers are welcomed.) I'd meet with this group of friends every Thursday for *juevecitos,* which translates literally to "the little Thursdays." Every week, we'd gather at a different girl's house to have drinks, eat, and catch up. We were loud, and 99 percent of the time, the night

Opposite
Part of the joy of fellowship with friends is cooking and preparing the table together.

Coming together brings the French joy, but it is also necessary for strengthening relationships among family and friends, connecting generations, and building communities.

ended in dancing and informal karaoke with no microphones. The weekly host was in charge of laying out a buffet of food, but sometimes we'd all pitch in by bringing a dish, or we'd order in tamales or tacos. Over the course of ten years, our group grew to thirty-plus girls (and two guys). When someone moved to New York from Mexico for an internship or a new job, a friend of a friend would connect them to us, and they'd join the *juevecitos.* We even used an Excel spreadsheet to organize our gatherings.

Since living among the French, I have learned that they share this same love of gathering. To the French *aussi,* fellowship is life. Coming together brings them joy, but it is also necessary for strengthening relationships among family and friends, connecting generations, and building communities. I daresay it's absolutely one of the most intriguing and important elements we can learn from French culture.

The French gather regularly. They rarely skip lunch. They often spend dinner during the week with their family around the table. On the weekends, meals are notoriously long. Oftentimes, *apéros* will extend into *apéro-dinatoires* (see "*Apéro* Cheat Sheet," page 111). Even when the French go on strike or protest—whether the issue is women's rights or proposed changes to the retirement age—it somehow turns into parades with music and drinks.

So, my life here in France has nourished that love of gathering that was instilled in me thanks to my Nigerian heritage and my induction into Mexican culture. In many ways, it has helped

encourage and ritualize gathering for me. It is part of my daily life now, and my raison d'être. Here, I've been allowed to figure out my own entertaining style, one that feels less intimidating yet incredibly inspiring. The French introduced me to *l'art de la table,* something I never experienced during those childhood gatherings, which featured paper plates, Tupperware, and tin foil. Through the French, I have been exposed to a whole new set of tricks and tools to elevate and enhance everyday gatherings.

When I was fresh off my Air France flight from New York, my approach to entertaining consisted of trying to be the "hostess with the mostess" and home chef extraordinaire. I had no friends, so I reverted to what I knew: trying to find a community and fellowship. As it was for my mother, inviting people into my home was a way to connect. But trying to be perfect made it messy. At countless dinners or gatherings, I spent half my time mired in details that didn't matter—like the Noah's Ark–themed birthday party I planned for my daughter, when I stayed up until four A.M. making tiny birthday hats for one hundred little plastic toy animals. (See "Kids' Birthday Parties," page 145, for more kid birthday party advice.) Or the many dinners that I served at ten P.M., which wouldn't have been a big deal in France, except that I had asked my guests to arrive three hours earlier, and I spent all those hours in the kitchen.

Opposite
We buy some ingredients from the market and some we pick from the garden, then everyone pitches in to help make lunch.

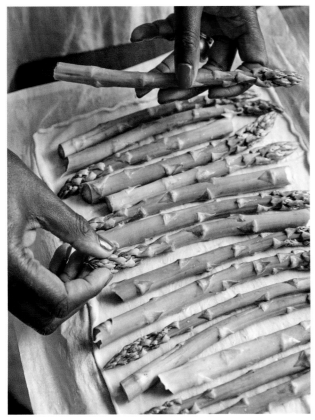

It took me a while—and a French friend asking why in the world I was going to such trouble—to learn what most French people already know: The purpose of entertaining is to bring together one's friends or family and spend time with them. Focus on the purpose: It should be a pleasure, not a pressure. The French keep their meals pretty simple, eat them sitting around a table, and stay at that table for a long time. Leave the fancy food for nights out at restaurants—especially if cooking is preventing you from being part of the evening's festivities—and keep the intention on spending time with your guests. Stock your shelves with dishes and bowls and platters you love and will actually use, so that no matter what you put down on the table, it will look beautiful and you will find joy in that moment. Sit with your guests, look around at these people you've invited into your home, take in the sound of the clinking glasses and plates, and you will truly feel you are living the good life. I do every single time.

Inspired by the words of Dr. Maya Angelou, I now focus on how people feel when they come to my house. As long as everyone feels welcome and enjoys themselves, I am happy to be the perfectly imperfect hostess. I am not a follower of strict rituals that make people feel excluded because they didn't attend any Madame Bougie's Etiquette School, because I sure didn't. Keep the focus on gathering and elevating the experience with beautiful objects.

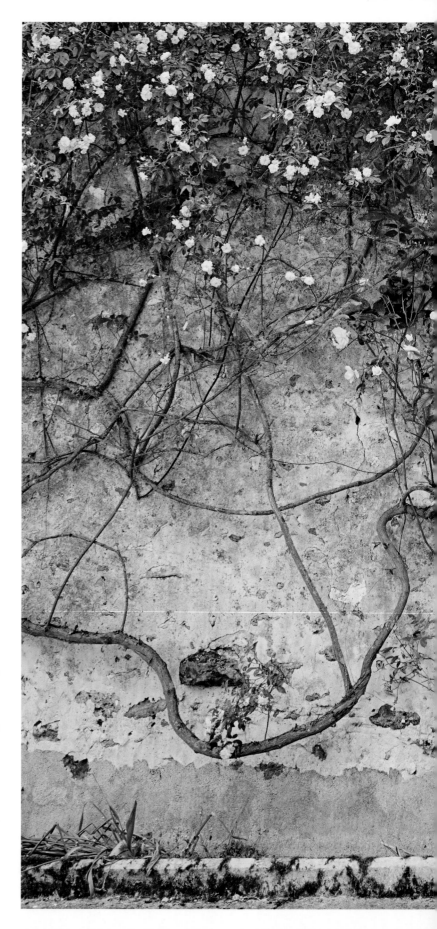

GATHERING THAT IS WORTH PROTECTING

In 2010, UNESCO recognized the French gastronomic meal an "Intangible Cultural Heritage of Humanity." Upon learning this, I immediately assumed the UN organization was classifying super haute cuisine. You know, cuisine that Francophile foodies will pay good money to eat.

But, in fact, it's more nuanced than that. According to UNESCO, the appellation is for more than simply a meal, but for everything that goes into the meal, such as buying the *bons produits* from local producers (see Lesson Two), selecting wine that pairs with a three- or four-course feast, and setting a beautiful table. In other words, it's the whole package and a sensory experience. The organization's website describes "the gastronomic meal" specific to the French as a "customary social practice" for celebrating milestones and achievements. (Although, I would argue that it's not only for special occasions.) UNESCO also distinguishes it as a "festive meal bringing people

Opposite

Inspired by the French, I make sure we sit at the table together as a family during the week as often as possible.

together for an occasion to enjoy the art of good eating and drinking. [It] emphasizes togetherness, the pleasure of taste, and the balance between human beings and the products of nature."

Now, that's what I call a practice worthy of protection! This encapsulates everything that I want from life: bringing together the people I love so we can experience *joie* in many different ways.

I especially love the phrase "the art of good eating and drinking," because it acknowledges that a good meal is something that has been sculpted over time, an art, over many generations, yet it's also something from which we can learn and build on.

Still, as much as I totally support this status, I had questions.

Why is it worth protecting?

Is a French meal any different from the meals I enjoyed growing up?

I needed answers, so I talked to a few French friends, all of whom offered variations on the same answer. The short version? Yes, the French gastronomic meal *is* worth protecting; it is a real thing (though most of my friends didn't remember or even know about the UNESCO status); and, yes, from the sound of it, it is quite different from my upbringing.

For starters, my French friends all grew up having simple meals for dinner during the week—but always with an appetizer, main dish, cheese with a salad, and dessert. My friend Tara's husband, Bertrand, a Parisian architect, says three courses are absolutely necessary. I wondered why he couldn't just sit down and have one main dish. "It's like a symphony!" he told me. "It's how we

structure the experience. It's also a way to eat a balanced meal. It's how we bring in vegetables from the salads and dairy from the cheese." My neighbor Raphaël, a Parisian photographer, says he also grew up eating various courses, but his mother kept it very simple during the week.

When I asked Raphaël why he couldn't just put food on the table to get his kid fed and off to bed, somewhat perplexed he responded: "Ajiri, it's not just food. It's dinner! We dine *ensemble.* That's the point." In other words, a dinner is not just about nourishment, but is a moment to *partager* (to share). In fact, Raphaël and his partner spend their entire days working while their son is at school. Therefore, a complete dinner at the table during the week is where they unwind, share. If they didn't have these moments at the table, he felt he would miss a lot in his family's life. He told me that his favorite memories from childhood happened at the table with his own parents, because they had nothing else to do but ask one another questions and share their days.

Things couldn't have been more different for me. I grew up eating in front of the TV more times than I care to remember. Sitting down at the table together wasn't a daily occurrence. Bertrand echoed the same sentiment. He told me that he felt disconnected and depressed when visiting his wife's family in the States: "No one cared about what they ate or indulging in this sacred time as a family." Similarly, Caroline, a marketing exec from the Pyrenees, whom I met through my Mexican friends, told me that when she visits her relatives

in the States, she finds it strange that everyone just grabs food and sits in different parts of the house or in front of the TV. "It feels like we're roommates, not family," she says. Bertrand told me, "*Les repas* [the meal] is the most beautiful moment for a family."

While I see their points, even as someone who loves a gathering, I often feel rushed during the week. Between post-school activities and nighttime rituals, I often want to feed my children quickly and get them to bed. But talking to my French friends gave me pause. It was time to reevaluate my evening rituals. I started sitting down with my family at the table almost every evening. (When we are out to dinner at a restaurant with friends, on the advice of Raphaël, I ask the babysitter to make sure to sit at the table with my kids at home.) I keep the meal simple during the week, and on the weekends, I try recipes from my favorite cookbooks. The kids love it, and I do, too! We all love this time to talk and laugh together, and I can already see my relationship with them strengthening. (And I now know all the elementary school gossip.)

Weekend meals, my French friends all said, tend to be decidedly more elaborate because the French have more time to devote to, say, simmering a boeuf bourguignon for hours or strolling the market for the ingredients and a bouquet of flowers to set on the table. When I moved to France, everything was closed on Sundays, and now I understand why. Everyone was at home preparing the big weekend meal. Raphaël and Bertrand, who visit their grandmothers' houses in the countryside twice a month, told me that their families tend to rotate their *recettes de grand-mère,* usually slow-cook

Opposite
It's important that the kids take part in setting the table and sometimes help with preparing easy dishes.

recipes like boeuf bourguignon, blanquette de veau, or a pot-au-feu. Caroline lived close to her grandmother, and they had the same big weekend meal every Sunday: roasted chicken and potatoes for lunch, oysters and salad for dinner.

And while weekend meals might be more elaborate in terms of time spent preparing them, they still bring the same amount of pleasure to all involved. Everyone I spoke to enjoyed the prep: shopping for the *bon produits* and talking to local vendors (see "What's So Special About Speciality Stores," page 83), discovering what was in season to inform the menu, and even discussing what to prepare.

All meals, says Bertrand, become a talking point. "In the morning, we wake up and discuss lunch. At lunch, we discuss dinner," he says, adding that, on vacation, he's even more hyper-aware about what he wants to prepare. "I like to spend the time to pick the right tomatoes, the right meat . . . it's a process, but pleasurable," he says. He also enjoys getting his children involved to help or even just to accompany him to the market, as he has a strong memory of doing so with his own father, something he wants to pass on to his daughters.

Transmission of tradition from generation to generation is something else the UNESCO designation highlights. In addition to following their parents to the market, French kids also help

Opposite
Serving simple strawberries in antique silver coupes makes dessert feel extra special.

out by setting the table, laying out linens, plates, cutlery, and glassware. This seemingly simple task allows them to contribute to the experience while also making them feel special and a part of the family. They learn how to dress a table, but also how to welcome guests. (You could say this is an early lesson for kids in gathering and modeling joy for them.) The table setting is an integral part of the meal because, according to Raphaël, "The food tastes better" when you set a nice table. Even if he orders takeout, he still sets the table using his own dishes, a practice Caroline upholds, too. She tells me, "Let's try to add a little fanciness to everyday life." Bertrand, whose grandparents taught him how to properly dress a table from flowers to candles, feels the same: "It's important to create a universe for your guests so they are *à l'aise* [at ease]," he says.

Still, the French people I meet are resolute in the belief that this protected tradition is not, by any means, a "gastronomic" situation. In fact, to them *gastronomic* is a marketing word. Rather, these meals are a way of life. And in that regard, I've come to answer my own questions about why these meals are worth idolizing. Being with people has saved me so many times, and life is meant to be shared, so why not do it over a meal around a beautifully set table? While I came to France with some semblance of fellowship with regard to meals and gathering as a ritual, looking at it in this new light has strengthened my resolve to uphold the tradition even further, and I urge you to consider doing the same.

A FEW TIPS FOR PREPARING A UNESCO-WORTHY MEAL

Plan your meal for the weekend, when everyone is more relaxed and available. Traditionally, Sunday is preferred, but Saturday works, too.

- This meal can become ritual or occasional; either way, invite your immediate family, extended family, friends, or people you want to get to know more.

- If cooking and dining on Sunday, shop the day before to buy fresh, local ingredients.

- Start prepping on Sunday morning.

- Lighten your load on the day of by setting the table the night before. Invite your guests to come at noon and start with an *apéro*. If you have children or an out-of-town guest, ask them to help set the table. Making the preparation a group effort is more convivial.

- Depending on space, mixing the kids in with the adults can be nice. Otherwise, create a mini-universe for the children at a separate table—and ask them for help in decorating it!

- If it's a daytime meal, lunch should start at around one P.M. with an appetizer, followed by the main dish, then cheese with salad, and last, dessert with coffee or tea.

- Dessert can be simple: fruit with Chantilly or something from a bakery.

- Don't rush! Your meal should be full of laughter and talking, so it might go on for two to three or even four hours. Remember, it's not just food. You are dining with people to share a moment. To share life and joy!

Opposite
Nothing is more joyful than a table full of food, family, and friends.

A CHAT WITH SUPPER CLUB HOSTS

LAURA ADRIAN AND BRADEN PERKINS
Co-owners of Verjus, Ellsworth, and Twenty-Two Club

If anyone knows the importance of gathering it is Laura and Braden, the dynamic duo behind the popular 1st arrondissement restaurants Ellsworth and Verjus. However, before they were restauranteurs, they were excellent hosts of Hidden Kitchen, a supper club they launched when they moved to Paris in search of community and connections. Turns out many people were in search of the joy that comes from gathering around a table, and a seat at their table quickly became a hard invite to get. They recently returned to hosting people at a new intimate table called the Twenty-Two Club, which overlooks the impressive Palais-Royal. They are the perfect duo to chat with about the importance of gathering at the table.

Q: Why do you think gathering at the table is so important?

[Laura] A: It's a nice time to unwind and reflect. To turn everything else off and focus on something that is essential, which is nourishing ourselves. We deserve to eat well and to connect and check in with one another.

Opposite
Laura and Braden in the Twenty-Two Club, overlooking the Palais-Royal.

Q: What prompted the move to Paris?

[Laura] A: Braden was a Francophile who was born in New Orleans, but raised mostly in the Boston area. He would come to France any chance he got because he loves the food and the culture.

[Braden] A: It's amazing! Just the idea that there's so many restaurants where you can go and there's a chalkboard of "entrée, plat, dessert" and it's around thirty euros for a meal that lasts three hours. It feels special to be rooted in such a deep and loving food culture.

Q: What inspired you to start your first supper club, Hidden Kitchen?

[Braden] A: We had moved here from Seattle where I was working in a restaurant and going to school full time. I had a group of friends from school, and a group of friends from the restaurant, and then suddenly we moved to Paris where we didn't know anybody. The idea was to use the supper club as a way to find some friends and meet some people. We said let's just invite some people to dinner and use that as a form of socializing. It very quickly pivoted into us being in the center of an Anglo food community [in Paris].

Q: How is the Twenty-Two Club different from your more intimate supper club?

[Braden] A: Well, for one we're in a stunning apartment, overlooking the Palais-Royal. And we're working with a lot of our own products, but also farmers who distribute to two-star and three-star Michelin restaurants—and we're still serving in our home. The ingredients have elevated infinitely from what we were able to find at the Bastille Market [for Hidden Kitchen] and then we have this team of cooks who have worked in two-star or three-star Michelin restaurants. It's the best of both worlds because we're doing a supper club, so we're communal, but we're getting products and teams that high-end restaurants get. Also, the kitchen is equipped with professional appliances like humidity-controlled refrigerators and dishwashers that operate in one-minute cycles. With Hidden Kitchen, we'd spend four hours the next day just doing dishes because we kept running out of hot water! It's very much like a professional kitchen, but in a residential setting.

Q: Now that you've been in France for sixteen years, is there a difference between hosting like the French versus Americans?

[Braden] A: There's one thing that's totally different when hosting a dinner with French guests versus Americans. Almost everybody else— Brits, Norwegians, Germans—give constant praise as the meal goes on. Whereas French people are almost always reserved until the very end.

Q: Have they come around to any of your American ways?

[Braden] A: There are a lot of French people who are interested in seeing the ways we're upsetting rules. People are excited to come experience the Twenty-Two Club.

Q: How do you find joie de vivre? What does it mean to you?

[Braden] A: For me, it's a hundred percent the products. I love being in a market. I love being on our farm. I wake up, have my cup of coffee, and I walk through the fields of vegetables. It's just so cool seeing what pops up and then thinking about how we're going to apply it to a new dish. When I get bummed out, I go in the kitchen and make something simple with lovely products. That snaps me back into it.

[Laura] A: Gosh, we just have such a nice life! But Braden and my dogs are my *joie*. Also, customers give me tons of pleasure. You do all this hard work so when people are happy, it just makes you feel like you're doing everything right. Serving people, and making them happy—a little bit drunk and full—that's really nice.

Q: If someone wanted to host their own supper club, what's a "must" for people at home?

[Laura] A: Hand somebody a drink the moment they walk in! It doesn't matter if it's nonalcoholic or alcoholic. Make them feel welcome, like they're taken care of, and help ease the pressure of being in a new place and meeting new people by putting something in their hands. It really is key.

[Braden] A: Just making sure that guests are well-fed.

Opposite

A long table prepared for guests, decorated with flowers from Laura and Braden's garden and antiques they've collected across France.

BON APPÉTIT!

The easiest way to make a French meal is to cook something seasonal, bought from your local producers. Don't overdo it, but also don't forget, if you are doing it the French way, that cheese is a must and that it comes *after* the main meal but *before* dessert. That being said, don't let the food keep you from the gathering. If you can't do three courses, then focus on one with dessert or with a pre-meal *apéro*. Here are a few suggestions to inspire your simple French meals.

APÉRO (NECESSARY EVEN AT LUNCH)

◊ Champagne, kir with cassis, Ricard, or Lillet

◊ Olives

◊ Oysters

◊ Charcuterie

◊ Raw radishes with salt and butter

ENTRÉE

◊ Tomatoes with mozzarella

◊ Roasted leeks drizzled with olive oil or a vinaigrette

PLAT

◊ Boeuf bourguignon served with baguette

◊ Coq au vin with roasted potatoes

◊ Blanquette de veau over rice

◊ Pan-fried fish in butter and lemon sauce

◊ Roasted chicken* with potato purée

* Really, anything that you can roast—just throw it in the oven and let it sit.

SALAD/CHEESE

◊ 1 to 3 different types of cheese

◊ Your favorite salad greens with a vinaigrette

◊ A fresh baguette

DESSERT

◊ Seasonal fruits with Chantilly

◊ Tarte tatin with vanilla ice cream or Chantilly

◊ Chocolate mousse with fresh seasonal fruits

Opposite
Sunday family lunch of tomato and mozzarella salad along with lemon basil roasted chicken and potatoes.

LINEN LOVE

In the early days of my living in France, most of the Parisian dinner parties I was invited to featured tables set with linens. I loved the way they felt: so light and soft. It didn't take long before I started spreading linen tablecloths of my own or tying napkins with twine or a ribbon to see how they changed the vibe of the table I was setting. It's fun to mix and play with colors based on a theme or design idea.

Eventually, in 2018, I decided I wanted to start making my own table linens. I researched various textiles and went to fabric shows. Then a friend told me her husband's family owned a flax farm, and she suggested I go visit. I've studied textiles, but I had never been to a textile mill to see the process. I jumped on this opportunity.

My son was only a few months old, so I strapped him to my body and roped my husband into a day trip to visit the Devogele linen farm in Chailly-en-Brie, in the Île-de-France. I walked through the flax fields and watched how the crop was processed and prepared. The Devogele family taught me everything about linen—and then announced that they had made lunch, so, of course I stuck around to eat! The table was set with beautiful linens, and they welcomed me, a stranger before that day, to their table. Ever since, I've been hooked on linens and the role they play in bringing people together at a table—even strangers.

If you want to elevate any moment at a table, don't forget the linens.

Opposite

In 2017, I put my son in the carrier and took a trip to a linen farm to learn more about flax seed, which is used to make linen fabric. It was here that I fell in love with linen textiles.

A LITTLE LIST ABOUT LINEN

- Linen is the only textile original to Europe.
- It's like wine in that the finished product is different every year depending on the rain.
- It's the most sustainable textile because it's used from tip to tail.
- It's made from flax, which is ethically produced, hypoallergenic, 100 percent biodegradable, and produces zero waste.
- Unlike other natural and cellulose fibers, which require irrigation and tons of water, flax needs only rain to survive.
- Flax is the only fiber originally from Europe and 85 percent of linen comes from Europe.
- Flax requires very little fertilizer and no pesticides or defoliants.
- Flax protects and fertilizes the soil, is grown from certified GMO-free seeds, and pulls carbon dioxide out of the atmosphere.
- Using linen means you are contributing to the movement for a more eco-conscious, healthier, and sustainable world.

SHHH! HERE'S A FRENCH SECRET

Opposite

A stack of linens from Madame de la Maison.

When it comes to using 100 percent linen fabric, some people are wary of the wrinkle factor. Personally, I find that it adds a nice texture to the table, but if you're a purist (yet still want to avoid busting out the iron), here's a little secret I learned from a French grandmother:

1. Wash your linen, remove it from the washing machine, and use your hand to smooth out the wrinkles.

2. Fold it while still damp and set it aside for an hour, or overnight if you're lazy like me!

3. Unfold it and hang it to dry if still damp.

4. If it is warm outside (or in your apartment) you can spray the tablecloth with a light spritz of water while it is hanging or on the table. Then run your hands over it to smooth the wrinkles, and watch your table cloth transform from wrinkly to wrinkle-free before your eyes.

Voilà! Your linen fabrics will be a little crisper and perfectly "ironed." For a softer look or feel, before you use them, toss them into the dryer with a damp cloth for fifteen minutes. (This is my preferred method, because I like the textured vibe. It will give your table that "I just threw this together," romantic look.)

only two hours and I was exhausted. And no one was all that impressed. The kids just chased me around asking for candy. And my daughter doesn't remember any of the work I did. Never, ever, ever again.

Remember: It's *your kid's* party! Let them have an afternoon of *joie* with their friends. Now, I either book a location that handles it all, or we do a picnic in the park with an *apéro,* a grazing board, and games.

The moral of the story is that kids really just want to play with their friends, open presents, and OD on candy. Let them.

KIDS' BIRTHDAY PARTIES

You know that saying "It's my party, and I'll cry if I want to"? Well, remember it the next time you plan a birthday for your kid that ends up being more about you than about them. During the first three years of my daughter's life, I did some crazy things. For her first birthday, I had a "Mini Me" theme and covered the table in about thirty different miniature versions of food: mini fried chicken sandwiches, mini burgers, mini hot dogs, mini grilled cheese with tomato soup . . . You get the idea.

For birthday number two, I clearly hadn't learned my lesson and turned my apartment's hallways, foyer, and dining room into Noomi's "Spring Garden Party," complete with about one hundred plants, which I had to send home with half the guests. I also served seven different varieties of tea sandwiches.

Birthday number three was the final straw. I stayed up all night to glue tiny hats and fuzz balls to the heads of one hundred little animal figurines for Noomi's Noah's Ark–themed party. I slept

HERE ARE SOME IDEAS FOR KEEPING IT SIMPLE AND JOYFUL FOR ALL:

- Book a place that takes care of everything.

- Arrange for a picnic in the park where kids can enjoy nature and feel free.

- Bake a cake if you want, or just order one and support a talented baker.

- For cookies, see the point above.

- In France, most parties are a drop-off event. Invite a friend or one parent you are close with to stay for a catchup.

- Cater if you really want to go all out or if you are celebrating a new baby and just need to feed the adults.

- Give out candy bags *at the end of the party,* just before you ship the kids back to their parents. (Sorry, not sorry.)

- Invite the parents to come for a drink and some nibbles at the end when they come to pick their kids up.

Opposite
Parc des Buttes–Chaumont is one of my favorite parks for birthday celebrations and picnics.

MODEL JOY FOR *LES ENFANTS*

When my daughter was four, and my French was still shaky, I remember sitting across from her teacher at a parent-teacher meeting, ready to hear that Noomi talks too much and is a bit rowdy. In fact, I even practiced in French what these sentences sound like so I could be ready with a rebuttal. But the first thing the *maitresse* Madame Bertich said was, "*Noomi a tellement joie de vivre. Vraiment. C'est superb.*" ("Noomi has such joy of living. Truly. It's superb.") I was shocked at this description of my daughter's comportment in school. She is a boisterous, chatty one for sure. But someone who possesses the joy of living? I wondered where she learned this.

As a foreigner raising two children in France, I am constantly amused and surprised at how their educational experience is designed to teach them to value and seek out joy in life. I didn't realize how much I played a hand in unintentionally teaching this skill set until my friend Zeva shared with me a powerful, and unusual, message from her son's fifth grade teacher at the beginning of the school year.

The teacher reminded the parents that scholarly education (reading, writing, math, et cetera) was his job. The parents' responsibility was to help their kids become more autonomous and to model happiness for them. It doesn't have to be verbal, he explained, but you can show them what a good life looks like for adults so they will want to create and experience that, too. I guess allowing my kids to be part of all my dinner parties and *apéros,* and even dragging them to the café with their coloring books when I needed a hot tea or glass of rosé post–flea market could be a good thing?

This message from my friend's teacher continues to inspire me to think about what non-verbal lessons my kids are learning from me and our daily life here in France. How am I modeling joy for my children? In Pamela Druckerman's bestselling book *Bringing Up Bebe,* which is about raising her kids in Paris, she discovers the French have a different approach. In the chapter "Tiny Little Humans," she explores the French belief of *awakening* as a kind of training for children in how to *profiter*—to soak up the pleasure and richness of the moment." I am fascinated by this emphasis on exposing children to things that will teach them to find pleasure in life. To *profiter*.

Raising children can—and dare I say *should*—be filled with far more pleasure than pressure. Instead of chasing, begging, or forcing children to do what we want, maybe we can approach child rearing in a way that's less restrictive and more free. Let's fill their minds with wonder and expose them to different foods, experiences, and ways of life beyond what's expected. More than anything, I hope to teach my children to always be in search of beautiful things, celebrate life, value fellowship with others, and find joy every day.

FRENCH-INSPIRED PICNIC

Picnics are practically a rite of passage for the French—from the kings and queens taking a break near Château de Chambord after a hunt to the Stan Smith—wearing teenagers who take their beers down to the Canal Saint-Martin. While I've been known to overdo it—bringing mini tables, foraging for flowers, and doling out assignments for who's responsible for pillows or a sun umbrella—all you ever really need is a blanket and a bottle opener. Oh, and maybe some silver dessert coupes, which make great wineglasses—but even those you can do without. Here's a little checklist for a French-inspired picnic.

- **LINENS**—both a large (blanket-size) one for your derrière and napkins for your hands.

- **KITCHEN TOWEL**—to wrap your bread or wipe off utensils.

- **CUTTING BOARD**—so you don't chop off a finger.

- **BAGUETTES**—must I explain? (Okay, see "A Bread Apart," page 74.)

- **EASY FINGER FOOD**—cheese, charcuterie, spreads, veggies, fruit.

- **SERVING TRAY**—this is really my own touch because I like to keep my drinks on a flat surface on the grass.

Opposite

I highly recommend keeping picnics simple, but I have been known to overdo it, like this picnic under the cherry blossoms at Parc de Sceaux when I launched my business.

DOS AND DON'TS OF A FÊTE À LA FRANÇAISE

IF YOU'RE A GUEST . . .

- **DON'T** arrive on time. You'll catch your host or hostess rushing around trying to finish up everything or get dressed.

- **DO** give them *un quart d'heure de politesse,* a "polite fifteen-minute-late arrival."

- **DON'T** wear your spikiest heels and risk never being invited back.

- **DO** be prepared to take your shoes off, especially if you arrive and realize they might destroy the host's parquet floor or cause the downstairs neighbors to shut the party down.

- **DON'T** show up empty-handed—ever.

- **DO** bring a simple gift like wine or a special condiment that can be shared or easily stored for later.

- **DON'T** refill your own wineglass. You'll be remembered as the overly "thirsty" guest.

- **DO** nudge the inattentive host and ask if they'd like another glass in the hope that they notice and pour you one as well. (If they don't offer to pour you another glass, it's pretty fair to pour your own glass after refilling theirs.)

- **DON'T** fill any glass to the rim. It's wine, not water. Fill it halfway.

- **DO** savor that wine rather than gulp it down.

- **DON'T** think you can just "pop in," or leave a French dinner early.

- **DO** be prepared to talk for hours about the state of humanity and go through many courses and bottles well past midnight.

IF YOU'RE THE HOST . . .

- **DON'T** assume everyone eats everything because . . . well, they don't.

- **DO** ask your guests if they have any dietary restrictions when you send out your invites,, so you aren't stuck feeling horrible or, worse, in search of an EpiPen mid-evening.

- **DON'T** serve fewer than three courses if it's a dinner party.

- **DO** make sure there is an *apéritif, entrée, plat, dessert,* and *digestif.* (In English, that's hors d'oeuvres, starter, entrée, dessert, and digestive.)

- **DON'T** trouble yourself making elaborate desserts unless you're a baker.

- **DO** support your local bakery and buy something delish and lovely.

- **DON'T** even think about not serving bread at a French dinner.

- **DO** serve bread in a basket at the dinner table. (If the carb avoiders don't touch it, then you'll have croutons the next day.)

- **DON'T** let there be silence.

- **DO** set the ambience with a playlist, candles, and low lighting.

- **DON'T** sip your wine or start eating until everyone has been served. (If you do, someone will look at you and say bon appétit, and they'll mean it sarcastically.)

- **DO** be patient while everyone clinks glasses and says "Cheers" and "Bon appétit" before digging in.

- **DON'T** apologize for any meal snafus. As Julia Child once said, "No matter what happens in the kitchen, never apologize." It's likely nobody noticed, and if they did, they wouldn't dare say anything anyway.

- **DO** cook something tried-and-true that you know how to prepare. The less fuss and chaos for you mean more time spent with your guests and enjoying yourself.

- **DON'T** hoard away the wine that your guests bring.

- **DO** allow your guests to show off and overanalyze said wine.

- **DON'T** serve an elaborate *apéro* that spoils the appetite.

- **DO** remember that an *apéro* is a prelude to a wonderful evening.

Above
Definitely do serve champagne before dinner.

DO USE THE GOOD CHINA

While I was growing up a skinny, knob-kneed Nigerian girl in Austin, Texas, during the 1980s, TV was my sacred source of education in becoming more "American." I loved watching family shows like *The Fresh Prince of Bel-Air, The Cosby Show, Family Ties,* and *Full House.* My two brothers and I would spend hours lying in front of the TV with our chins propped on our knuckles and our eyes glued to the screen.

It was from the kids on these shows that I picked up style tips and new words and learned how families in the United States functioned. The families on those shows were so different from my own—especially during dinnertime. All the kids and their unforgettable, quirky friends— Cockroach, Jazz, Cornflake, Kimmy Gibbler, and of course, Steve Urkel—never passed up the chance to join the family at the set table. Occasionally, an oddball relative would also pop in for dinner, and a lively conversation would ensue. I loved the joy, conviviality, and the swell of emotions that came to the table. There was something special about all those people sitting together talking, laughing, and sharing thoughts. I treasured the mixed generations and personalities

as well as the friendships, the big reveals, and even the denouncements.

I appreciated the beautifully orchestrated chaos of different arms reaching across pretty china strewn about a lovely tablecloth. I wanted to mimic the adults who clinked silver cutlery to a crystal glass before making an announcement. And I remained fascinated by the ritual of slapping a fabric napkin on the table and storming off as a means of declaring drama.

Things at my house looked a bit different from what I saw on TV. When I came home from school, a giant pot with some strongly scented Nigerian dish was usually sitting on the stove, calling my name. While we had extra family members floating in and out of our homes, none of our American friends wanted to stay for dinner, as we weren't serving any American classics.

When hunger crept up, I would walk past my mother's dark wood cabinet of treasured china on my way to the kitchen. It was full of shiny things I was forbidden to touch. Through its glass doors, I could see ceramics and antique finds from my mother's Saturday garage sale trips, as well as her precious wedding china. Half of it was on display, and the rest of it was packed away in padded containers. The cabinet drawers were velvet-lined and contained sets of elegant flatware with gold accents running along the handles.

These treasures haunted me on that daily walk to the kitchen, because I was always instructed to use Tupperware instead. Routinely, I'd ask, "When can we set the table with the pretty china?" Her response was always: "Not today. I'm waiting for a special occasion." I never gave up asking, and she stayed true to her response.

One year, we were hosting Easter with many of our Nigerian friends from church. I figured this would be classified as a special occasion. (Never mind that Nigerians gather to celebrate darn near everything, including a graduation to middle school.) Wearing a pastel-colored, frilly version of my Sunday best, I reminded my mother that it was Easter, which meant the Lord had risen, and that *this* was a special occasion. As a devout Christian, she couldn't deny my liturgical reasoning and granted my wish. (Maybe the dress helped?)

Together, we set our family table for twelve. It was a glorious ritual I will never forget. I joined my mother in setting a plate in front of each chair and placing the appropriate cutlery beside each plate. I followed her naturally graceful effort, placing the items slowly and ceremoniously to savor this moment she was sharing with me. After we were done, we stood back and looked at the table together. It was marvelous. I immediately became lost in imagining my TV sitcom moment. (But I ignored the part where an Easter ham would sit on the table next to fried goat meat and *foofoo*.)

Eventually, I was brought back to the present by the sound of my mother clearing the table and returning my porcelain dreams to her precious cabinet. I watched in horror. What was she doing? This new reality was confirmed when she closed those dark wooden doors, and the china disappeared behind the ivory knob. She told me she had decided not to use the good china for

Easter lunch, because someone would probably break them. Instead, we had lunch with our guests on paper plates and out of Tupperware.

I was devastated, but I never gave up asking to set the table like that again. Still, her response remained equally unwavering: She was waiting for a special occasion. Sadly, it never came, and my mother passed away when I was twelve years old. Only a week before, perhaps sensing that her time was nearing its end, she pulled me into her bedroom and told me that soon all the beautiful china would be mine and that I could set the table with it whenever I wanted. This remains one of my saddest and most vivid memories and is the impetus for my always using "the good china"— because my mother never did.

I promised myself I wouldn't make the same mistake, and neither should you. Every day is worthy of "the good china" and all the other pretty pieces you buy. (And "the good china" can truly be a metaphor for anything you love.) You may have chosen them for their beauty or story and, therefore, they bring you joy. So, what are you waiting for? You deserve to use them. When you welcome someone to your table, share your treasures with them, you're offering them a gift. Why buy antiques and special pieces only to lock them away in a dark cabinet? Whether you want to bring people together for memorable moments, like on the sitcoms of my childhood, or you're just enjoying a quiet dinner alone, these occasions are deserving of your best pieces.

Don't be like my mother and wait for a day that may never come. Every day is a special occasion, so bust out all your table treasures.

Opposite
These nineteenth century *rose terre de fer* plates from the legendary manufacturer Saint-Amand et Hamage were one of my first finds when I moved to Paris.

CHEESE ETIQUETTE

I don't like to be snobby about etiquette rules, especially if they might make a guest feel uncomfortable, but knowing how to properly cut cheese is a fun party trick.

ROUND: Cut these like a cake, into small triangles from the center out.

SQUARE & WEDGE: Cut in lengthwise slivers, but don't ever slice off the nose (aka the tip)!

ATYPICAL SHAPES LIKE HEARTS: Start in the middle and cake it up again.

PYRAMID SHAPES: Cut these like a cake, too, into long, narrow slices.

CHEESE IN A WOODEN BOX: These are usually heated, so scoop it up with cutlery.

I always say there is power
in gathering around a table
because it is where our
souls collide.

L'ART
DE LA TABLE

I was once featured in *Frederic* magazine, a
publication created by the textile and design
company Schumacher. In the article, the journalist
hilariously wrote, "If you have a Michelin-worthy
feast at Aki's, it is most likely beautifully plated
take-out." I couldn't help but crack up. While this
isn't totally accurate, it isn't wrong, either. I might
serve beautifully plated takeout . . . or I might
cook. It all depends on how I feel. But the point is
that I stopped trying to make five-star dishes years
ago. I now focus my energy on spending time
with guests and setting a stunning table. I love all
the little accessories and details that go into table
setting. As my friend Bertrand says, *C'est le petit
touch qui fait la différence.* "It's the little touch that
makes the difference." Setting the table inspires
your guests and sets the mood.

THE TABLE is deeply symbolic and is used in
everything from art to politics to daily life.
Throughout history and in art, it's been
a place where people come together to
laugh, to cry, to feed, to imbibe, to sign
treaties, to . . . do everything! To create,
to destroy. I always say there is power
in gathering around a table because it
is where our souls collide. At a table,
we inspire one another, share with one
another, connect with one another.

I FIND PLEASURE and take great pride in
the act of designing a setting. It's my art. I
love playing with plate colors, shapes, and
napkin configurations. Be creative!

SMALL ADDITIONS—knife rests, napkins,
and name card holders—can make a huge
difference in a table's overall essence.

NO TWO GATHERINGS are alike. It's all
about playing around with ideas and being
crafty and clever. Personally, I do this by
balancing colors, mixing and matching
plates or glasses, and manifesting an
entirely new table setting—even if just
one small detail is different.

TABLE STYLING doesn't have to be elaborate,
over-the-top, or intimidating. Try choosing
just one special element to set the tone.

RESEARCH TELLS US that when it comes to
design, we are happier when function
meets beauty. So, choose pretty plates
and cutlery that will make the food more
delicious and appetizing.

TIPS FOR TAKING CARE OF SILVER

Silver gets a bad rap because it seems so pesky to care for, when really all it needs is some TLC. Here are a few tips on caring for your favorite silver pieces.

- In a nonreactive container of enamel or porcelain, soak your items in hot vinegar for fifteen minutes. Use enough vinegar to cover them completely before rinsing them under warm water and drying them with a clean cloth.

- To remove stubborn stains, rub gently with a paste made of baking soda and vinegar. And always dry straightaway with a soft, lint-free cloth to avoid leaving water stains.

- When you aren't using silver serving pieces, maintain their shine and slow down the oxidation process by wrapping them in cling wrap or storing them in Ziploc bags.

- While silver cutlery can go in the dishwasher, it should be removed as soon as the washing cycle has finished and dried by hand to maintain its shine.

- If you prefer to wash your cutlery by hand, use warm, soapy water immediately after using it. It's not ideal to let food form crusts on your antique cutlery overnight. And don't use detergent containing lemon or any other citric acid, as this might damage the metal.

- An effective (if slightly wacky–sounding) method is to clean your cutlery with ketchup. A few drops on a paper towel should be enough to wipe away the tarnish. Rinse with clean water and then dry carefully with a soft, lint–free cloth.

Opposite
Tables of silver at the flea market in Paris.

TABLE TALK

Nobody likes awkward silences at a party. Whether you're a host or a guest, sometimes you need a few conversation starters to get things going—or coolers when things need to be simmered down. I love to make sure everyone is happy, engaged, and acquainted—and you will, too. The French, especially, love a little *dispute*—argument, debate, heated discussion. *Disputer* is almost a national sport, and it still makes me uncomfortable, so feel free to clink your crystal wineglass and lighten the mood with a question-and-answer game.

As a guest, you'll also want to have a few talking points in your pocket; you don't want to immediately ask someone what they do for work and then spend hours talking about that. The subject can be dreadfully boring, and the question is sometimes seen as invasive or unimportant. If you are really curious about what someone does, it will usually reveal itself in conversation as they share their story. Here are some ways to start the chatter—and stop it when necessary!

CONVERSATION STARTERS

◊ "Where are you from?"

◊ "How do you know [insert host name]?"

◊ "How long have you lived in [insert city where you are]?"

◊ "Have you seen any good movies or TV shows recently?"

◊ "What's a good podcast or book you could recommend?"

◊ "Have you listened to the new [insert musician's name] album?"

◊ "What was the last live concert you attended?"

◊ "Do you have any favorite restaurants in [insert city name]?"

◊ "I love your [insert clothing item or accessory]. Where did you get it?"

CONVERSATION COOLERS

◊ "What's your deepest desire at this very moment?"

◊ "If you could live in any decade or year, when would it be?"

◊ "If you could eat the same meal every day for the rest of your life, what would it be?"

◊ "What are three items you would take with you to a desert island?"

◊ "If someone handed you a million dollars today, what would you do with it?"

◊ "What is something that moved you recently?"

Opposite
A lively, long lunch at my friend Vanessa's house that was packed with endless conversations.

THE SEATING GAME

To assign seats or not to assign seats is often the question. As a promoter of joy and a lover of little details, I always favor prearranged seating. It's one less thing for people to (awkwardly) think about. After all, since you know your guests best, take a moment to enjoy thinking about where to place people in order to foster new connections.

If I could seat any guest around a table, it'd be based on the following criteria:

◊ **Someone who will make everyone laugh** with inappropriate jokes and lighten the political chatter, like Trevor Noah.

◊ **A good storyteller** who can inspire all the guests, like Oprah.

◊ **A pair of best friends** to bring lots of laughs and inside jokes we all want in on, like Amy Poehler and Tiny Fey.

◊ **Women who have experienced amazing careers** with stories to share and **who might be up for spontaneous karaoke** after dinner, like Dolly Parton or Tina Turner.

◊ **A therapist** who can give us all great advice—and maybe spill stories on their clients—like Esther Perel.

◊ **Someone who has a good opinion on everything,** like Fran Lebowitz.

◊ **A journalist** to spark heated political talk that will then need to be calmed down with a conversation cooler, like Christiane Amanpour or Anderson Cooper.

◊ **A friend who can inspire us by her chic style and important work,** like Amal Clooney.

◊ **A daughter of legends,** who therefore must be full of stories, not to mention tales from their own impressive careers, like Charlotte Gainsbourg or Tracee Ellis Ross.

◊ **An avid reader** to talk about the latest books we've read and to suggest ones we should add to our shelves and **who would also be up for karaoke or charades** after dinner. I'm thinking Reese Witherspoon.

MUST-HAVES

Beautifully set tables often come with lots of "extras," but there are a few things that I absolutely couldn't host without including:

1. Bread baskets

2. *Salière et poivrier*—salt and pepper shakers or bowls

3. Wine coasters

4. Knife rests

5. Low candle holders

6. Lots of vases of various kinds

TABLE CENTERPIECE IDEAS

One of my pet peeves with regard to dining is having to strain, duck, and dive to see or speak to the person across from me—which is why, when it comes to centerpieces, I like to keep them low. Save your candelabras and tall flower arrangements for a buffet, or put them on side tables, and use votives for a seated dinner. Here are a few other suggestions for my fellow drama queens and those who like to keep it simple at the center of the table.

FLOWER PETALS: Sprinkle your table with the petals from flowers that have passed their prime or ones you've dried yourself, or buy dried rosebud tea and sprinkle away. It's romantic and a tad messy, but very dramatic, and it makes the table look special.

FRUIT AND VEGGIES: Citrus fruits and root vegetables make excellent table runners, depending on the season. (If you cut the citrus fruits open, the smell is divine, and you can use them later for juice.)

BUD VASES: These are my favorite go-tos for adding flowers to a table. Play with different shapes, heights, and sizes, as well as flower types in the same color or different shades. You could also do lots of simple wildflowers—which are cheap, chic, and cheerful.

VOTIVE CANDLES: Use these to add ambience and drama—especially if you're dining outdoors. If the votives are set inside a glass or jar, you won't have to worry about the wind blowing out your spark. They're a simple way to add an elegant mood to an everyday dinner table.

ON BEAUTY

FIND ELEGANCE EVERYWHERE—IN ITEMS,
SPACES, AND PLACES

Below

The stairs and exterior of the recently renovated Musée Carnavalet, which focuses on the history of Paris.

Previous page

Féau Boiseries, a private archive of historical wall panels.

A thing of beauty is a joy for ever: Its loveliness increases; it will never Pass into nothingness.

—*John Keats, "Endymion"*

THE JOY OF THE ARTS

I studied the decorative arts in New York City, choosing a program that would allow me to focus on two of my passions: costume history and interiors. The degree itself, while a mouthful to say—master of arts in the history of the decorative arts, design, and culture—was a holistic approach to studying for me. To understand why people wore what they wore, or designed what they designed, I also needed to understand what was happening in the world at the time that might have influenced those decisions. In other words: I needed context.

Another way to define the decorative arts, according to the ole *Merriam-Webster,* is "art that is concerned primarily with the creation of useful items." So, essentially, artistic items besides fine art (painting) and sculpture that serve a purpose—such as architecture, ceramics, costumes, textiles, furniture, gardens, and objects. In our coursework, we used a methodology known as "material culture" to look at, discuss, interpret, and understand the objects and spaces that reflected a society and the cultural times. For example, the discovery of King Tut's tomb in 1922 captivated the world and seeped into designs in the way of scarabs in jewelry, pyramid- and obelisk-shaped objects, gold lamé in fashion, and running geometric patterns.

Even before I began creating a life in France, the country fascinated me with its proliferation of design, objects, and creation in the decorative arts. My formal studies helped me gain a deeper understanding of my passions, and the tools to make connections. France, as I discovered in class and even further once I relocated, is highly concerned with taste and beauty. The two are also very much linked with power and culture. Look at Louis XIV, for example. He imprisoned his cultural minister, Nicolas Fouquet, for throwing a housewarming party that showed off his amazing taste in design, which the king saw as a threat to the monarchy. He then took Fouquet's entire creative team—the architect, landscape designer, and painter—for his own project in Versailles.

That same Louis, also known as the Sun King, was obsessed with France's image, but really more with others' perception of him as an erudite, tasteful, artistic, yet powerful leader. He commissioned works by the best artists and invited noblemen to witness these and then spread the word about how fabulous the king's court was. He surrounded himself with only the best of the best.

In the *Fabrication of Louis XIV,* author Peter Burke notes, "It was commonplace in the 17th century to observe that magnificence had a political function . . . was considered to be impressive, in the literal sense of leaving an 'impression' on viewers like a stamp on a piece of wax." In other words, the Sun King used art, culture, and what he deemed beautiful to impress the world and evoke pride in locals.

In a way, he was diffusing culture. The French have a word for this: *rayonner,* "to spread or shine." Clearly, France does this exceptionally well—and is quite intentional about it, too. The French are proud of their accomplishments, especially in the decorative arts, and they want to share this with the world at large. Look at the world's fairs.

To love beauty is to see light.

—*Victor Hugo*

These were the epitome of France's *rayonnement,* the place where they exhibited and propagated their industrial artistry, demonstrated the strength of their economy, and elevated their national pride. An early example of such *rayonnement* was in 1867, under Napoléon III, when they opened Parc Montsouris and Parc des Buttes-Chaumont, proving that comfort and leisure were the new ambition and pride of Parisian society. And in 1900, the Belle Époque and art nouveau styles were on full display courtesy of buildings and monuments such as the Pont Alexandre III, the Grand and Petit Palais, and the Gare d'Orsay (now an art museum), not to mention the city's Métro entrances designed by Hector Guimard.

French presidents ranging from Charles de Gaulle to François Mitterrand appointed cultural affairs ministers—such as writer André Malraux, who launched an initiative to preserve the heritage of France by cleaning the soot off great buildings and established theaters and cultural centers in smaller cities so that everyone could have access to culture. Jack Lang was another famous minister of culture; it was he who launched the now-annual Fête de la Musique in the 1980s, a daylong street party and celebration of music that has been adopted throughout many parts of Europe.

France even has an artist status known as *intermittent du spectacle,* which protects the likes of musicians, cinephiles, writers, painters, and others. These professionals work a certain number of hours per year, and the government pays them a salary for the remainder of it, so they have time to create. Can you imagine? The government pays artists money just to be their beauty-delivering, joy-creating selves.

Seeking beauty and engaging in culture in France are encouraged by other such designations—"Most Charming Village," "Flowery Village," and "Most Remarkable Garden"—celebrating everything from architecture to green spaces. France is heavily invested in its citizens' health and happiness and will help them find it in beautiful objects and culture. So, if you want to find joie de vivre like the French, engaging in culture and the decorative arts is a good place to start.

In our times, when doom and gloom pop up when we haven't even asked for it, who doesn't need a daily reminder to seek out the stunning? A 2011 study published in the British Medical Association's *Journal of Epidemiology and Community Health* indicates that engaging in cultural activities such as visiting a museum, attending a music concert, going to the theater, lingering in a garden, or creating art has profound effects on your health and well-being regardless of wealth or education status.

As a student and lover of history, I view France as a playground for discovering elegance in antique objects, gardens, architecture, and interiors. As John Keats wrote, "A thing of beauty is a joy forever." Like the French, I find beauty in things and spaces that are deeply imbued with the past. I am fascinated by the never-ending joy they provide. Beautiful things, and even the memory of them, stay with us day after day and year after year. They make an impression on us, and we, in turn, can access their beauty for our limitless joy.

WHAT'S OLD IS BEAUTIFUL AGAIN

Every Saturday, from the time I was six years old, my mother dragged me to garage sales early in the morning. I would climb into her red Dodge Ram pickup truck, and we would drive around the neighborhood looking for makeshift cardboard signs with arrows pointing to a yard or garage sale. "One man's trash is another man's treasure," she told me. At first, I rolled my eyes and dreaded these outings. I found it embarrassing to dig through other people's castoffs. The worst was when we pulled up to the home of someone in my class. I didn't want to be the Black kid in school wearing a classmate's old stuff! It didn't help that there were zero other Africans in our community and only five other African American families. Racism was subtle yet rampant in Austin, Texas, in the early 1980s.

Looking back now, I see my mother's thrift trips as an unintentional primer for my fondness for flea markets and antiques. (Isn't that always how it is? How do our mothers know?) I must've been eight when I slowly started to see these moments with my mother as privileged time together and also as a way to find beauty and purpose in something aged or no longer wanted. We weren't exactly plucking out high-priced antiques in the suburbs of Austin, but my eyes got an early apprenticeship in searching for beauty that others might miss or can no longer see.

When I moved to Paris, I immediately sought out the various ways people shop secondhand. There is the *vide-grenier,* which translates to "empty [your] attic." These are closer to an American garage sale, where everyday people get together with their neighbors and friends to sell things they aren't using anymore. And people really do empty their attics and closets! At a *vide-grenier,* you can find everything from a grandmother's dinner service (yes, please!) to old toys (maybe) to electronics from the 1980s (no, thanks). But you have to be ready and willing to dig. A few professional sellers sneak into these sidewalk sales, but mostly the antiques pros have their own brick-and-mortar stores or they sell their wares at a *brocante,* one of the ephemeral flea markets that pop up on different streets on the weekends, or an antiques fair called *foires,* which are organized throughout the year. There are also more permanent areas where stalls are rented and antiques are sold year-round. The two most popular in France are the Puces de Saint-Ouen, on the edge of Paris and in the town of L'Isle-sur-la-Sorgue, in Provence.

I love trolling all these spaces, from the seemingly junkier and free-form variety to the more organized and well-heeled. For some reason, right from the get-go, these worlds were way more exciting to me than Texas garage sales because they were full of French people's castoffs: eighteenth-century *terre de fer* (ironstone) dessert stands, art deco serving platters, hand-painted Quimper plates, Victorian cutlery, and blue-and-white *paysage* tea sets. I'm a history nerd, and I geek out on finding something created in another era for a specific reason and then repurposing it for a use that fits my time and modern needs. Being able to recognize that an item adorned with shells might be a rococo or Revival style brings me great satisfaction. But maybe there's an element—a color, a textile—that I'm unfamiliar with. I find an equal amount of gratification by googling or going through my personal library to research a piece's origins. I am motivated by this balance of recognition and uncertainty.

I am not alone in this. The French love to stroll through *brocantes* or visit *les Puces.* They even have a specific verb for this: *chiner,* meaning "to hunt or bargain shop." I see so many generations of people sifting through tables of antique plates, old glassware—clinking them to learn if they're crystal or glass—digging through boxes of antique linens, walking from stall to stall. I have run into friends or even made new ones just strolling through a *brocante.* When the sun is out, the vibe is energetic and contagious. Sometimes there is music playing from a vinyl record stall or a live band performing for tips. Around lunchtime, vendors sit around a table in their stand to enjoy some wine and a meal they brought from home or picked up from a nearby restaurant. That's usually my cue to take a break from shopping and have lunch at a nearby café or brasserie.

My friend Maxime is a devout *chineur,* which is someone who loves to search for treasures in a flea market. We met through our kids, who are in the same class. Maxime grew up in Narbonne, is an ex-professional sailor, and now works in sports marketing in Paris. Nothing about him screams "I love a good antiques market." In fact, I had initially pegged him as just a sports guy, and was surprised to learn about his love of *brocantes* and *vide-greniers.* When he found out I wanted to start a business reselling French antiques, he sent me information about flea markets and offered to come along.

He tells me that if he has friends in town, or wants to impress a girl, he always takes them to a flea market. "I feel like it's a representation of my culture and my past," he says. And whenever he visits other towns, he looks for flea markets or antiques shops, because he feels it's a way to connect with a place and its locals.

When visiting other peoples' homes in France, I always notice how many antiques there are—maybe they have objects passed down from their grandparents or found at a flea market. It is clear the French appreciate the idea of breathing new life into the past, in celebrating what came before to appreciate the present. For me, it's also about stories. Every object has one. Knowing that someone previously used and loved an item before I wove it into my life brings me great joy. I love being able to look at something on my shelf or a table—say, a hand-painted casket jewelry box where I unearthed a diamond hidden deep in its corner; or a pair of faceted art deco vanity jars— pick it up, and be immediately transported to where or how I found it. These meant something to someone, and now they mean something to me.

Sadly, and perhaps ironically, all my mother's treasures were put into trunks and boxes after she passed away and shoved into a storage unit when I left home for college; they have since disappeared. It breaks my heart that I don't have any of her favorite finds, but I like to imagine they ended up at a garage sale or secondhand shop and that someone came along and found in them "stories" from the life my mother and I shared together. There's beauty in that, for sure.

Opposite

At street flea markets there are tables full of antique silver serving pieces and crystal glasses.

When I asked him about this fascination, he told me that although he's been going to *brocantes* and *vide-greniers* since he was a teenager, and more regularly in his early twenties as a weekend activity to look for items for his apartment, the point wasn't necessarily to buy anything. Rather, Max finds strolling flea markets a social and even romantic activity. He enjoys walking the markets with friends just to look and be inspired. His parents had a little shop in Narbonne, where he grew up experiencing a small community vibe among shop owners and regulars. Markets today give him that same feeling. There is the energy of people looking and talking. In fact, there's even a sense of intimacy, given that people are selling their own belongings. People are excited to discuss the history and meaning behind the objects they're trying to resell. Put simply: Max feels good being there.

3

FLEA MARKET OBJECTS I COLLECT THAT MIGHT INSPIRE YOU

6

KNIFE RESTS (1) are great for protecting linens from getting extra soiled, but also for resting serving utensils at a buffet. I collect **STRAY COFFEE AND TEA SAUCERS** (2) and use them as plates under soft-boiled eggs, as a sauce dish, or for sushi or pot stickers. **NAPKIN RINGS** (3) are a sweet detail on a table setting and **NAME CARD HOLDERS** (3) are a lovely way to seat your guests, identify items on a buffet, or prop up a quote or card you love on a mantel. I use **TART AND DESSERT SERVERS** (4) for serving all kinds of desserts, frittatas, as well as savory and sweet tarts. **APOTHECARY AND OIL JARS** (5) of all shapes and sizes make beautiful presents, but they're also perfect bud vases. **SERVING TRAYS** (6) make wonderful gifts because they can be engraved. You can also use them next to a bed, on a bed, on a table, or at a picnic.

TEN TIPS FOR ANTIQUE SHOPPING

I can't tell you how many times friends, family, and strangers have told me they find shopping for antiques intimidating. Or, they ask me how I find so many beautiful things while they struggle. I admit that being *à l'aise* (at ease) with antiques hunting has taken time, knowledge, research, practice, and, most importantly, patience. It's a hobby that has turned into work. I get a thrill from hunting, but I feel joy day in and day out when I see or use my found treasures at home. I love shopping for clients, going with friends, and taking groups on tours if it means helping others find something special, something full of history and of the unknown or untold stories eagerly awaiting a new owner to transform its tale. Here are some tips for DIY antiques shopping (see "More Sources of *Joie*," page 264, for my favorite places to shop):

1. **USE YOUR IMAGINATION.** Look beyond what the object once was and imagine how it can serve you today.

2. **FIND PERFECTION IN THE IMPERFECT.** The imperfect bits give antiques character and make them unique. Of course, it's important to inspect pieces before you commit—especially textiles. But embrace the patina on copper or silver objects; even small chips on ceramics are okay. These are signs of use. Plus, you can reupholster or polish any damage or imperfections you don't want to live with.

3. **DON'T BE AFRAID TO ASK FOR A BETTER PRICE.** In France, you ask, *Est-ce que c'est possible de faire un petit prix pour moi?* which literally means, "Is it possible for you to make a little price for me?" It's a cute and polite way to ask for a price reduction. They expect you to ask—in fact, most items are priced with wiggle room in mind. And if you buy a few things from the same vendor, they're likely to give you a bigger reduction.

4. **DON'T LET AN ITEM BE THE ONE THAT GOT AWAY.** Know what you want to pay for something, but if you walk away from it, understand that the object might be gone forever. I used to worry that I was being scammed on prices. Now I know what I am willing to pay for something. There are items I sold to others that I wished I had kept for myself, and I may never find another like them. I know now that if it's something that brings me great pleasure to use and own, I will willingly pay a pretty penny for it.

5. **SKIP SOME STANDS, BUT DIG DEEP IN OTHERS.** Sometimes just wandering around is enough for your eye to catch inspiration and hook a hidden gem. And while we all love the organized shops, you'll find good deals when you dive into random boxes, old trunks, and messy tables. The less organized a shop, the better the prices.

6. **TRUST YOUR GUT.** If something looks too shiny and new, then it might be. (For example, the nails in "antique" furniture are a dead giveaway if something is new or has been refurbished.) Sometimes the presence of dust and dirt is good. The item might have been sitting tucked away, waiting for you to come along and snag it.

7. **EDUCATE YOURSELF.** The internet is full of articles on how to identify silver-plated versus sterling, porcelain versus stoneware, earthenware versus faience, transferware versus hand-painted. I don't think one is better than the other, but just knowing the difference will help you feel more confident in the market. Bonus: I also think it's fun to educate yourself about the different design styles and their iconography and ornamentation. It makes spotting something more exciting. Also, collecting art books or visiting museums and châteaux will help you learn what you like and train your eye to seek certain things.

8. **THE EARLY BIRD GETS THE GOOD ANTIQUES, BUT THE LATE BIRD GETS BETTER PRICES.** When packing up and returning home with their unsold wares, dealers prefer a lighter load. Personally, I like to get to a *vide-grenier* or *brocante* early, break for lunch, and then stroll around in the afternoon.

9. **BE PREPARED AND DRESS COMFY.** Wear comfortable clothes and shoes; you might be on your feet all day. My outfit consists of flats or sneakers and a fanny pack or crossbody bag. I like to have easy access to my money, which is usually cash, and I want to avoid back or shoulder pain. I am also a hard-core antiques shopper, so you might bump into me with a wagon or a cart on wheels. That said, a tote is totally okay. Don't forget a tape measure, and keep your room measurements handy!

10. **GET TO KNOW YOUR DEALERS.** They love sharing information about a piece and will negotiate with you. Talk to them about what you're looking for—they love the hunt as much as you do! In fact, they might already have something hiding in their stock or will find it for you.

CREATE YOUR OWN STORY AT HOME

British textile designer William Morris once said, "If you want a golden rule that will fit everybody, this is it: Have nothing in your house that you do not know to be useful or believe to be beautiful."

I live by these words.

My family's apartment in Paris is the first place I've lived, since I was twelve, that truly feels like home. It's where I love to welcome friends, family, neighbors, and even strangers. I walk around it and feel immense happiness and pride for what my husband and I have created together with our children. It's not simply a space I quickly decorated and filled solely for functionality or show, but a home full of memories and of pieces I love that spark joy.

For example, it brings me joy to sit on the reupholstered Louis XV armchairs we found at a flea market set up along a river in Dordogne. I love walking past the lithograph, marked "#24/50," that I picked up in the Puces de Saint-Ouen hoping it was secretly a Matisse masterpiece; the signature can't be easily identified. I love the black matte wood 1950s sideboard with etched-glass doors full of my continually revolving and never-ending collection of crystal glassware I've picked up at markets all around France. Then there are my bookshelves, which my handy Swiss husband built to stand on either side of the early twentieth-century marble fireplace with its gilded mirror. They're full of books from my life in New York, all color coordinated and mixed in with others I picked up from exhibitions or at the English bookstores on the rue de Rivoli near the Louvre. I love the old wooden table made from condemned railroad ties that I found by chance during my first months in France. It's usually where I place one large or several tiny vases with the week's fresh flowers. And in the entryway, I love my collection of antique mirrors from different design eras above a bench we built and covered with toile de Jouy fabric.

To some, these items are just "stuff," material objects. But to me, they're memories and history that is unique to us, and therefore, they make our house a home. These pieces tell a story, and while my story may still be unfolding, they bring me comfort and *joie* in the process.

Opposite
My apartment in the center of Paris is full of my antique finds and objects that bring me joy.

AN ODE TO NATURE AND GARDENS

In my New York days, I visited the city's parks and gardens a handful of times—maybe not as much as I should have, in retrospect, but enough to appreciate their gloriousness in the center of the concrete jungle. During lunch breaks, when I worked at the Museum of the City of New York, I sometimes sat with my colleagues at Central Park's Conservatory Garden. And I loved to stare out the window daydreaming about my big life plans while riding the bus across the park en route to my internship at the Metropolitan Museum of Art's Costume Institute.

I've always found beauty and inner peace in gardens, but a survey of landscape design lecture in grad school brought things to a whole new level for me. In the lecture, we dove into the history, elements, and materials of different types of gardens (English, Japanese, Moorish, and French). We were asked to consider how the landscape contributes to or participates in fostering national and/or regional identity. We pondered the designed landscape and how it improved society as a whole.

In France, designed landscapes were historically one of the ways to showcase power for the monarchy and nobility. What we know as traditional French formal or baroque gardens are actually a copied inspiration from Italian Renaissance gardens of the seventeenth century, thanks to Catherine de' Medici. The gardens showed the power of man's mastery of nature, but also his superiority of skill, wealth, and knowledge. Louis XIV, for example, could show off to the world that he had a garden for hosting a thousand guests. In doing so, he could also prove that he had a staff to *maintain* that garden: skilled artisans who brought in water for fountains and clipped hedges. But these garden spaces were reserved for the wealthy and those privileged to be in their company.

Nowadays, in France and beyond, gardens are exceptionally important to those living in urban environments—where not everyone has a green space of their own. We can go to gardens to get inspired, but also to improve our oxygen intake and overall health. A 2015 study published in the journal *Landscapes and Urban Planning* found that just by walking through nature, study participants experienced less anxiety and more positive emotions. That's right. A quick pop into a park or a stroll down a tree-lined street will not only boost your energy level and creativity, but also help slow your heart rate, lower stress, and bring you a moment of joy. Research suggests that you can even get some of these benefits simply by imagining yourself in nature or looking at pictures of it.

The journal *Environmental Science and Technology* encourages environmental policies that create green spaces in urban environments to increase health benefits. Since 2014, the mayor of Paris, Anne Hidalgo, has been on a determined path to improve the quality of life in the city and expand these kinds of spaces. But far before her, we can thank Napoléon III for deciding that designed landscapes weren't only for the privileged. With Baron Haussmann, he developed the Parc Montsouris; the Buttes-Chaumont, one of my favorite parks in the center of the city; and the much larger forests—the Bois de Vincennes and the Bois de Boulogne, on the western and eastern edges of the city. He wanted to create beautiful spaces for Parisians, but also show what his government could do for the people. (Again, and still, flexing his power.)

What I love the most about French gardens are what's called their "elements of surprise." During my first trip to Versailles, with my graduate class back in 2006, we were asked to describe our initial impression of the garden just outside the château. We all remarked that it was, indeed, quite beautiful. But then we walked down those steps, and suddenly there was so much more than what initially met the eye. Behind those tall hedges was a mini amphitheater with waterfalls! And next to a giant manicured bush was a tall sculpture that, perhaps, had been obscured when we'd looked down from up above. These are the elements of surprise. When you view a French garden from above, you see one thing, but when you get down into it, you are, essentially, Alice in Wonderland. The whole thing is almost an illusion. It keeps going on and on, and you see new things at different levels and, perhaps, with each return visit. You take a step and think you've reached the end, but then you turn right or left, and there's a whole other element—a labyrinth, even!

As is to be expected with such wildly elaborate flourishes, maintaining a French garden is not for the faint of heart. All that snipping and clipping to keep order might be better left for trained gardeners. The rest of us can enjoy and appreciate what has already been established and maintained for centuries, and improve our mental or physical well-being, by merely taking a late-afternoon run around a reservoir, practicing yoga under a shady tree, or enjoying the simple sight of a rose in bloom.

Above
The Medici Fountain in the Jardin du Luxembourg.

- Château or house (main focus)
- Topiaries (balls, cones, obelisks)
- Parterre in the form of labyrinths or designs like a *parterre de broderie* (bed forming an embroidery–like pattern)

- Symmetry, geometry
- Gravel and/or stones
- Water (fountains or reflecting ponds
- Decorative additions (statues; urns; large pale–pink terra–cotta planter pots; columns)

- Simple color patterns (lots of green, white, pale pink, lavender)
- Spaces for relaxation and reflection, with benches or iron garden furniture
- Allées (walkways)
- Bosquets (thickets)

ELEMENTS OF FRENCH GARDENS

Listen, we can't all be André Le Nôtre, the landscape architect behind the gardens of Versailles (among others). So, if you're a city dweller like me, plant lavender on the balcony (if you're lucky enough to have one), take care of a little olive tree, or pot a tiny boxwood. These are all easy ways to bring a little bit of beauty and a dose of the slow, contemplative (yet powerful) French joy to your domicile. But the next time you're in France, impress your travel companions by calling out some of these typical French garden elements.

STOP AND SMELL (OR PLANT AND DISPLAY) THE FLOWERS

When I lived in Texas, fresh flowers were only reserved for special occasions: romantic gestures, anniversaries, weddings, and funerals. I don't remember any flower shops in our suburb, but the supermarket sometimes sold carnations mixed with baby's breath. In our own garden, my mother grew pink and red rosebushes in the front yard and tulips around the trees and leading up to the front door. Cutting her precious flowers was totally forbidden, so I don't remember ever seeing a single flower in a vase in our house. In fact, I'm pretty confident we didn't own vases.

In New York, in my twenties, my floricultural and horticultural horizons expanded because designer showrooms always had at least one big, beautiful (and expensive) arrangement. Bodega bouquets were also plentiful, but they also resembled my suburban supermarket varieties, which didn't excite or inspire me very much.

It wasn't until I moved to Paris that I started incorporating flowers into my life on a weekly

basis. In Paris, you can't walk down the street without passing a *fleuriste*. They're almost as plentiful as bakeries and definitely as popular as eyeglass boutiques. From fancy floral designers to family-run businesses, each arrondissement blossoms with a variety of florists who line the sidewalks outside their small shops with petals and stems of all varieties. Even in the rest of France, when I drive through little villages, right along with the sole village *boulangerie, boucherie, pharmacie,* and *institut de beauté,* there is usually a flower shop. You will also always see a flower stand at almost every farmers' market—in fact, this is probably where you'll get the best deal. While most people grab a *botte* (bunch) and arrange them back at home, some stands at the market will make a mixed arrangement, too.

In contrast to how I lived in the States, now I grab flowers on a whim. But, more often, I gift them to my friends. If I like getting flowers, why wouldn't they? In fact, ask anyone in France what is the best gift to bring to a dinner party, and they'll almost always say, *Les fleurs!* Why? Depending on whom you're visiting, they might want to choose the wine themselves and have a preferred bakery for bread and dessert (as we know by now), so flowers will most definitely bring a smile to their face.

Incorporating flowers into your daily life is an easy way to surround yourself with beauty, whether you casually walk past them en route to another room, catch a whiff of them on your bedside table, or read a book among them while lounging on your terrace. But it's a guaranteed moment of shared joy when you buy them for someone else. The special occasion? Nothing more than life itself and your quest to bring beauty wherever you are or to whomever you care about.

Tip

The next time you plan on bringing flowers for your host, consider having them delivered the morning before or after a dinner party, so your host doesn't have to scramble looking for a vase while juggling coats and pouring drinks.

HOW TO BRING MORE FLOWERS INTO YOUR LIFE

- Buy flowers on your way home because you had a good day (or a bad day) and deserve them. Pull over on a country road and pick wildflowers to decorate your home.

- Pick up a bouquet on the way to a friend's house.

- Grow some flowers or herbs at home in your garden or on your terrace.

- Take a workshop on flower arranging.

- Use foliage, grass, or the extra bits that are usually used as fillers as the main focus for your decoration.

- Save and recycle glass jars (from jams and syrups) or empty wine bottles to use as vases.

- Be your own florist by buying a bunch of bouquets and creating mini arrangements for your next holiday meal.

- Actually stop and smell the roses (or lilacs or hyacinths or any other fragrant flower) the next time you walk by a bush in the wild.

- Flip that bouquet upside down to prolong the flowers' beauty by drying them. Rid them of their leaves first, let them get crunchy for four weeks, and then spray them with hairspray to set.

A NOVICE'S GUIDE TO FLOWER ARRANGING

I am not a professional florist or designer, but over the years I've discovered unique and less conventional ways to play with, and display, flowers. First tip? Start buying the foliage, fillers, and strange–looking buds. You don't need to break the bank. Cheap and cheerful go a long way. The more you experiment and play, the better you'll get and the more personality your arrangements will have. Try new flowers, repeat old ones, dry them out, work with only a single color and foliage, or even just a single flower—the world is your *Tradescantia spathacea* (oyster plant). Also, you don't have to stick to traditional vases. There are other vessels with which to enjoy and display flowers. Here are a few materials I use quite often:

- Little antique apothecary or oil jars for small bouquets

- Water pitchers and cans for casual arrangements

- Silver chalices or champagne buckets for short stems and big blooms.

A CHAT WITH A GARDEN GURU

AMY KUPEC LARUE
American in Paris, garden tour guide, and private florist

Amy Kupec Larue moved to Paris from Boston more than thirty years ago and is now the queen of flowers and French landscape design in the city. She has worked for more than four American ambassadors, arranging flowers for their events and their private residences. She now hosts private and group botanical tours all across France. Talking to Amy, whom I call anytime I need a garden-based location for a shoot, makes me feel like a student again. She is so knowledgeable and generous with her information.

Q: When I moved here, I felt that most French people had a heightened interest in flowers and gardens. Why do you think that is?

A: It's definitely true, and it struck me as well. In an urban environment, I think it's all the more vital, because you're surrounded by streets and tall buildings, so you want to have that little corner of nature *chez toi,* and you do it by bringing home a bunch of tulips or roses. When I first came here, the height of chicness was to send a bouquet the day before or the morning of the dinner party, so that the hostess would have time to use them as a centerpiece or set them in the *salon.*

Opposite
Amy in the gardens at Parc de Bagatelle.

Q: Did you buy flowers regularly prior to living in France?

A: As soon as I could walk, I was picking flowers. I was always attracted to them, and I regularly pissed off my mother, because I was cutting flowers from her garden. As soon as I got to be a teenager, and I was driving, I would pull over on the side of the road to cut wildflowers. I would pull down grape vines and make wreaths using a lot of grasses, branches, buds, even leaves.

Q: How can people who don't live near a garden or who don't grow their own learn to appreciate them as a thing of beauty?

A: Start small, start simple, and buy a different bouquet of flowers every week. Watch what happens to them. This is what I did. Having not studied flowers or gardens or anything like that, I had no idea what flowers had a long life versus ones that only lasted two days. I had to learn from my mistakes. It was purely observation. Hit or miss.

Q: What's your favorite thing about the French "element of surprise" in a garden?

A: They hide all kinds of things in there. In a way, they prove you wrong. You don't know everything. You don't see everything until you actually walk through the gardens. Then you realize, *Oh my gosh, there's a staircase there.* And then you go a little bit further and there's a stream. They are individual spaces, and sometimes it's overwhelming. But by closing off sections, you have these little enclaves, and then you step inside and there's a fountain or a statue or a little room that is just for you. A lot of people don't actually go behind those high green walls to discover what's in them.

January called [*Lonicera*] *fragrantissima*—it smells so amazingly good. In January! When there's nothing going on in the garden, you have these tiny white flowers that'll knock your socks off.

AMY'S FAVORITE GARDENS BY SEASON . . .

WINTER: Jardin des Serres d'Auteuil—It has all these indoor greenhouses with different ambiences. There is a whole greenhouse dedicated to the pineapple family!

SPRING: Jardin Albert Kahn—"because of the cherry blossoms."

SUMMER: Parc Floral—"There's quite a lot of shade, and you have classical music concerts in July and jazz concerts in August. You can hear it from anywhere in the park, or buy a ticket to get closer to the stage. They also have twenty-eight pavilions peppered throughout the garden, including two with bonsais. So, you step into these alternate worlds with these collections of plants, and it's also great because it's shaded."

FALL: Parc Montsouris—"because of the trees."

ANYTIME: If you're after a "four-seasons garden," one that's lush anytime of the year, Amy suggests *Bagatelle,* out in the forest; *Jardin des Plantes,* in the 5th; and *Luxembourg,* which she says "is great for the ambience, the cafés, and the people-watching."

Q: What are different ways to experience a garden space?

A: You could have picnics, meetings, or read. It can be very active, or it can be very sedentary. It's not just your eyes that are working in a garden. All of a sudden, your nose is picking things up, and your ears are picking things up, because you can hear the rustle of leaves. Even bamboo, when wind blows through it, has a beautiful sound to it. There may be gurgling water or a big fountain splashing water. If you walk on acorns or leaves, you'll hear them crunch underneath your feet. I'm also very touchy-feely in a garden. I know what leaves have scents now, and I run my hand across a leaf, and it'll very often release some essential oils. Suddenly, you're smelling orange blossoms that came from a green leaf or these teeny tiny flowers. There's a honeysuckle that blooms in

LOOK UP AND AROUND: BUILDINGS OF GRANDEUR

In Paris, I am confronted with history and opulent design on a regular basis while doing everyday activities. One day, I might drag my daughter out of the house, walk past the art nouveau Métro signs designed by Hector Guimard, which were both loved and hated in their time, descend into the underground only to eventually arrive in front of the grand Beaux-Arts Palais Garnier, home to the Opéra National de Paris, built at the request of Emperor Napoléon III in the nineteenth century. As a musical theater junkie, I can't help but think of *The Phantom of the Opera* as my eyes take in the building's façade, with its columns and its gilded statues, odes to the art's greatest creators, among them Mozart and Beethoven. If I'm lucky enough to go inside to drop my daughter off for a birthday party—yes, the Palais Garnier is a destination for kids' birthday parties—I'll remind myself to book another tour or get tickets to see a performance for a peek at Marc Chagall's fresco inside the theater.

Back outside, I turn around and inhale the grand avenues designed by Baron Haussmann, admire the symmetry, and continue running my errands. I might take a taxi to meet a friend for lunch in the Marais—but traffic is a nightmare, so I jump out and decide to walk the rest of the way. In doing so, I weave through cobblestone streets, pass a few beautiful giant doors (built that way so horses could eat), and then stop in front of one of them to take a picture.

Then I take a shortcut through the arches of the Place des Vosges, glance up at the wrought iron gates with their golden tips, walk past Victor Hugo's old house, and then grab a bus down rue de Rivoli to sit at Le Mimosa, a restaurant near the Place de la Concorde, a square that is chock-full of striking monuments—most notably, the Luxor Obelisk, carved from a single piece of red granite, and a gift to France from Egypt.

Even heading to my therapist in Montmartre provides a feast for the eyes. Her building features a beautiful wrought iron gate, and the entry has the most stunning floral art nouveau mosaic tiles in pastel colors.

J'habite à Paris (I live in Paris), which is an incredible outdoor museum.That said, the capital isn't the only place in France with admirable architecture. I often seek out structures all across the country—from the Renaissance châteaux in the Loire Valley to the three-arch stone Pont Julien, an impressive Roman bridge in Provence dating back to 3 B.C.

In Paris and beyond, it's all here for you: medieval, Renaissance, modern, millennial, the

Opposite

The Lavirotte Building in the 7th is an exquisite example of elaborate art nouveau architecture from the early 1900s.

old interlaced with the new.

In 1926, French fashion designer Jean Patou wrote in an article in *Harper's Bazaar,* "To be modern does not mean to upset and revolutionize . . . a modern style is not a style which forgets all tradition of the past and from day to day pretends to impose a new rule. To be modern is to have the thought, the tastes, and the instincts of the epoch in which one lives. A modern art is, therefore, an art which is adapted to the taste and to the needs of its era." While he may have been speaking about fashion, his sentiment applies to all art forms. Patou, who presumably viewed himself as a modern man, was explaining that modernity does not mean a complete rejection of the past. He believed that every style, during the period it was created, was modern and contingent on its reflection of the culture. He declared, "Almost all the stages of French art have been, each in its turn, modern epochs."

Whether I'm purposefully on the hunt for inspiration or just doing errands, I always make it a point to stop and appreciate where I am and the structural styles that came way before me—and that will last long after I'm gone.

A CHAT WITH A BEAUTY & DESIGN CONNOISSEUR

ALINE ASMAR D'AMMAN
Lebanese–Parisian architect and founder of
Culture in Architecture

Aline Asmar d'Amman is a Parisian interior architect who grew up in Lebanon and has worked on impressive projects, such as the redesign of Le Jules Verne, the restaurant in the Eiffel Tower; Les Grand Appartements with Karl Lagerfeld at Hôtel de Crillon, and the Palazzo Donà Giovannelli in Venice. I first learned about her through reading *The New Parisienne: The Women and Ideas Shaping Paris,* a book by Lindsey Tramuta in which we were both featured. When I read Aline's profile there, I was completely enamored by her grace, accomplishments, and overall chicness.

My fantasy and fascination with this woman became a reality when we co-hosted an event and I stepped into what is probably the most breathtaking office in all of Paris. Art books, classical sculptures, marble slabs, crystals, fabric samples—these strewn-about objects are not just for inspiration and beauty. Rather, they're all part of Aline's work. Her office is like a living, breathing museum and Aline, with her trained eye and curious mind, is its fabulous curator-in-chief. What's more, the space itself has an enviable view of the city.

While working with Aline, I saw firsthand her passion for talking about travel, spaces, and places. Here, she shares her thoughts on finding beauty daily to inspire her in life and work.

Q: Why are beautiful spaces, homes or interiors, and gardens so important?

A: Beauty is a body and soul healer. Our interior spaces are havens of immaterial emotions that protect and uplift the spirits. They massage our skin, eyes, and inner being with gentle sensations of gratefulness and mindfulness. Objects have a soul and a presence. If you cherish them, they will comfort you with stories to be told for generations.

Q: Where does your passion for beauty come from?

A: I was born and raised in Lebanon, a country where years of adversity were followed by a hopeful reconstruction, so I learned to find beauty in ruins and in the tense contrast between the precious and the raw. I learned to cherish imperfections and combine them with a certain ideal of humanistic resonance. I was motivated to become an architect by the certainty that good design makes the world a better place.

Q: How do the French prioritize beautiful things and places?

A: The French champion the layering of old and new, curiosities and rarities. They've also mastered the art of transforming beauty into a very distinctive art de vivre. Karl Lagerfeld taught me this when we realized the interiors of Les Grands Appartements at Hôtel de Crillon, mixing tradition with modernity.

Q: Speaking of, why do you think it's important to blend the old with the new, in terms of both interior objects as well as architecture styles?

A: The old soul loves to feel rejuvenated with contemporary creations. Understanding the history and heritage of buildings, monuments, and decors is key to feeding the narrative of the new designs: relevance and bold storytelling are part of what I seek when working on a project because with a true narrative you can never go wrong. It also has to do with respecting the past, embracing legacy, and falling in love with imaginary characters.

Q: Can you share some tips and tricks for making something old feel new and fresh?

A: Context is everything. It's about the balance of drama and minimalism. Don't let go of your oldies—isolate them rather than stacking them all together. Play with the contrast of the unexpected. Mirrors, for example, add depth and reveal new perceptions. A clean mirrored wall behind an old console, flanked with a pile of books, kicks in a new vibe. Inversely, a hand-carved vintage mirror on a white wall introduces character and charm.

Q: Let's talk about those oldies. What draws you to flea markets?

A: The thrill of the hunt! Sourcing for our design projects is when the magic happens. During the many months or years it takes to finalize and deliver a site, the journey is punctuated with visits to the antiques markets and discovering one-off treasures we didn't think we needed. Objects with scars transform a room. They are conversation points and become familiar family members who diffuse an infinite mystique to every living space. What also excites me is the human encounter with the sellers who dedicate their lives to finding treasures. The quest for beauty comes alive with their stories.

Q: What about an object will catch your eye?

A: The strange and broken is a powerful magnet. I am attracted to the inherent narrative; the story that lies behind the creation. It's what I hoped to share with "The Memory of Stone" collection, my first series of functional sculptures, tables, and consoles that mix reclaimed slabs of rare marbles and scarified Vicenza Stone slabs. Texture and time bind together man-made memory and spontaneous beauty. I am always hunting for unusually shaped crystals in enchanting colors, too. They represent a glorious gift from the earth with millions of years' energies captured in their sparkle. Beyond their astounding beauty, their healing properties and energy are palpable and real.

Q: It must be hard to choose, but do you have a favorite building in Paris?

A: Maybe it's an obvious choice, but the Eiffel Tower holds a special place in my heart. I was lucky to work with Michelin-starred chef Frédéric Anton, who dared to start from scratch on a blank canvas for the entire layout and interior design of Le Jules Verne restaurant. It was a thrill to strip down the space and build a contemporary stage for his haute cuisine, weaving perspectives inside out and inviting the "City of Light" to the table. Each of the bespoke textures, materials, shapes, and designs pay tribute to the Iron Lady and Gustave Eiffel's engineering. But above all, it's a nod to Paris's elegance—and to women! Such thrills are difficult to compete with, but if there's any other building that holds a special place in my heart it's Versailles. Pure French *savoir faire*, both in architecture and design.

Q: Can you share some of your favorite hidden gems in Paris?

A: The dazzling Parc Monceau colonnade, La Naumachie, is a feast for the eyes. When being restored in the eighteenth century, it was conceived to look like ruins. There's the Le Défenseur du Temps in the Quartier de l'Horloge, in Le Marais, where a four-meter brass clock is protected by fighting a dragon against a crab and a bird. It imbues allegories of earth, sea, and sky, and always steals my heart. Another precious clock, with its royal blue and gold ornaments on stone, appears on the façade of the Palais de la Cité—and it's been working since the fourteenth century!

Q: What brings you *joie?*

A: I am fortunate to have three men in my life, my husband and two handsome boys. Being with them, a pile of books, and the sound of the Mediterranean shores could be the definition of *joie* for me. But I wouldn't be complete without a helmet and heels, long hours sketching, and designing alone or with my wonderful team at the office. My true *joie* comes from the balance of motherhood, creative accomplishments, and being surrounded by an ever-growing group of like-minded and fearless women who are relentlessly striving to shape tomorrow's world.

Opposite

La Naumachie in Parc Monceau is one of Aline's favorite hidden gems in Paris.

Following page

The Marie Antoinette Suite in Hôtel de Crillon designed by Aline.

CHÂTEAUX AND GARDENS GALORE

I must have lived in a château in a previous life, because I feel so drawn to their grandeur, and I never tire of visiting these beauties across France—most of which also have magnificent gardens. Whether Gothic style with soaring ceilings and dark wall tapestries or Renaissance style with fairy-tale turrets and drawbridges, these former palaces are fine examples of French design and well worth exploring. Here are some not to miss.

CHÂTEAU DE CHAMBORD. Located on the eastern end of the Loire Valley, this massive castle is known for its Renaissance architecture, including a famous double helix staircase designed by Leonardo da Vinci that allows visitors to ascend and descend without ever passing each other.

CHÂTEAU DE CHENONCEAU. This Loire Valley beauty spans the Cher river (thanks to an exquisite gallery bridge) and was a source of contention between King Henry II's mistress Diane de Poitiers (to whom he left it) and his widow, Catherine de' Medici.

CHÂTEAU DE VERSAILLES. Quite possibly the most famous in the world, and a designated UNESCO World Heritage site, this royal residence was home to all the Louis, most notably the Sun King, Louis XIV, whose emblem can be seen throughout the palace and gardens.

CHÂTEAU DE VAUX-LE-VICOMTE. An underrated gem located about thirty-four miles outside Paris, this baroque château is where superstar landscape architect André Le Nôtre, who designed the Versailles gardens (and many after that, including the Jardin des Tuileries in Paris), got his start. It is one of the best examples of a seventeenth-century garden.

CHÂTEAU DE CHAUMONT. This lesser-known gem, located in between the towns of Blois and Amboise, along the Loire River, is actually a hand-me-down. Meaning: This is where Catherine de' Medici banished King Henry II's mistress Diane de Poitiers. But it's no dump. In fact, built in the year 1000, this turreted beauty is now host to France's annual International Garden Festival and is a center for art installations.

CHÂTEAU DE VILLANDRY. Described as a "country house," this former ancient fortress in the Loire Valley, now in Renaissance style, features one of France's most magnificently manicured gardens, with fountains and topiaries galore. Back in the day, though, it was where royals came to broker peace—most notably, King Philip II of France and Richard I of England.

Don't stop at visiting the well-known châteaux. There are so many more to explore and I highly recommend you also check out the gardens listed in "More Sources of *Joie*" (see page 264).

Opposite
Château de Chambord.

Following pages
(222 and 223)
Château de Chenonceau;
the gardens at Château
de Versailles.

HISTORICAL GEMS IN MODERN-DAY PARIS

Paris is full of historical gems from the past, many of which have been painstakingly maintained for centuries to inspire us today. Here's a map of those worth seeking out the next time you're looking for beauty "hiding" in modern-day Paris that will add a little spark of joy and wonder to your day.

In 1901, the **LAVIROTTE BUILDING,** at 29 avenue Rapp, in the 7th (designed by French architect Jules Lavirotte), was unsurprisingly awarded the Best Façade by the city of Paris. A rare surviving example of exquisite and elaborate art nouveau architecture, the building features undulating and sinewy ornamentation of femininity and nature and animal themes in wrought ironwork, sculptures, and ceramic tiles.

A quick pop into a park or a stroll down a tree-lined street will not only boost your energy level and creativity, but also help slow your heart rate, lower stress, and bring you a moment of joy.

CASTEL BÉRANGER, at 14 rue Jean de La Fontaine, in the 16th, is the work of Hector Guimard, known for his art nouveau Métro signs. This site is acclaimed as the founding construction of the art nouveau movement.

The entirely residential RUE MALLET-STEVENS, in the 16th, was inaugurated in 1927. The rare artistic work of a single architect, Robert Mallett-Stevens, the street's structures are a great example of interwar modernist architecture, which can be seen in everything from the houses to the street signs, resembling abstract sculptures or cubist art.

HÔTEL DE LA MARINE is not a hotel, but rather a mansion and former palace that eventually became home to the French naval ministry before being turned into a museum in 2021. It now displays the former (and very fancy) apartments of the royal Garde Mobile (aka the king's decorators and architects). In France, approximately two hundred of the top artisans worked to restore this space using eighteenth-century methods.

Inside the MUSÉE GUSTAVE MOREAU, the former home of a symbolist painter and professor at the École des Beaux-Arts de Paris, there's a stunning spiral staircase made of cast iron and wood. While Moreau himself, who actually taught Matisse, was relatively unknown during his life, he prepared this space to become a museum after his death.

Designed by Armand-Albert Rateau, The Musée des Arts Décoratifs features French couturier JEANNE LANVIN'S PERIOD ROOMS (boudoir, bedroom, and bathroom), which are a prime example of the height of art deco. (The museum also has nine other period rooms from different eras.)

A visit to the FÉAU BOISERIES showroom and workshop, which are by appointment only, for lovers of design and history is like visiting a candy store. You want to touch and take everything home. It is like stepping through time to walk the halls of some of the most fascinating French tastemakers. You can run your fingers across the wall panels from Jeanne Lanvin's 1930s living room, gaze at the panels from Napoleon III's living room, get inspiration from panels that Fragonard painted for a famous courtesan, and drool over the fireplaces of Edith Piaf and Marie Antoinette. The designs ranging from extravagant seventeenth-century boiserie to early twentieth-century plaster and gold foil are a history lesson and inspiration in how we can bring these creations into modern-day decor.

Hiding inside the École Nationale Supérieure des Beaux-Arts de Paris, on the Left Bank, is the **COUR DU MÛRIER,** a courtyard that is open to the public but most people don't know exists. It is a former cloister of the Petits-Augustins convent founded by Queen Marguerite de Valois.

The **DOUBLE HELIX STAIRCASE INSIDE THE BOURSE DE COMMERCE,** a newly renovated building dating back to 1889 and currently housing François-Henri Pinault's art collection, is a rare type of staircase. It consists of two sets of stairs that allow people to ascend or descend separately and never cross paths. (The only other staircase of this kind in France is the one designed by Leonardo da Vinci, at the Château de Chambord.)

While the **EIFFEL TOWER,** built by Gustave Eiffel for the 1889 Exposition Universelle, is one of the most famous historical gems in Paris, a good place from which to view it is the simple steel, but grand, **PONT DE BIR-HAKEIM.** From its inception—pun intended; *Inception* is one of the many movies in which the bridge has appeared—it was meant to be a pedestrian footbridge for the 1878 world's fair, but it was destroyed and rebuilt in 1905 by Jean-Camille Formigé as a two-story bridge to accommodate pedestrians, cars, and the Métro. (Bonus: From the bridge, you can access the man-made Île aux Cygnes, created in the 1820s.)

The Beaux-Arts **PONT ALEXANDRE III** is a well-known bridge in the center of the city and another world's fair submission—this time from 1900. Because of its arched shape, building it was an engineering feat at the time, and all the glamorous gold ornamentation was really used to hide the excessive structural supports then needed. At the 1925 world's fair, the bridge was closed off and lined with shops displaying the top luxury products of couturiers, jewelers, and *fourreurs* (furriers). The bridge's placement was intentional, to show the curve of the Seine, but more important, to provide a dramatic view from Les Invalides to the Petit and Grand Palais, which were also unveiled at the 1900 world's fair.

Above
The Pont Alexandre III, one of the prettiest bridges in the city.

Following page
Rue Mallet-Stevens in the 16th arrondissement.

ON SELF-CARE

LOVE YOURSELF À LA FRANÇAISE

Caring for myself is not self-indulgence,
it is self-preservation . . .

—*Audre Lorde*

FEELING GOOD IN MY OWN SKIN

I moved to Paris with green contact lenses camouflaging my dark brown eyes and a seven-hundred-dollar weave. I wanted that superstar-meets-supermodel look. Up until that point, and throughout my twenties in New York, I had lusted after luscious, flowing locks like Beyoncé's and the long, lean body of Naomi Campbell. (I tried all the fad diets to attain that body, including drinking only water with lemon and cayenne pepper for a week. It was awful, and I was in a rotten mood for days!) What's more, I hated my wide nose and gap teeth and spent hours researching possibilities to change them. I also splurged on designer clothes—and by "splurge," I mean I spent my rent money. Yet, monthly spa treatments or a solo wellness trip seemed extravagant and a bit self-indulgent. It's no wonder I was continually searching for *joie:* I never felt satisfied with myself or my life as it was. I was trying to find, and buy, it in all the wrong places.

Fast-forward to living among the French for more than ten years, and I have shaved my head, replaced my designer dress obsession with a passion for antique plates, and changed my mind about going under the knife to modify my nose. I also don't want to starve myself by participating in torturous fad diets or have a massive closetful of fashion that no longer fits or makes me feel good.

I am now happily a work in progress, gradually adopting the self-care attitude of the French—which is that style, beauty, and overall well-being are derived from pleasure (not the guilty kind), preservation, and feeling *bien dans ma peau*—or "good in my own skin."

Thierry Wasser, head perfumer at Guerlain, says, "Beauty is not about changing or disguising yourself. It's about changing how you feel. It's about attitude. It's about revealing yourself . . . your true self. Skin care, makeup, and perfume are for your own pleasure. And if you believe it has an effect, your skin is going to be beautiful and you're going to look how you feel."

Self-care *à la française* is boosting your own confidence by being neither a slob nor a slave to fashion trends that don't represent your true being. Self-care *à la française* is not working yourself into the ground and then talking about work when you aren't, in fact, working. Self-care *à la française* is taking a vacation and giving in to things that bring you pleasure. It's doing absolutely nothing. It's saying no. It's gathering with people for wine and nibbles to laugh and connect—and not feeling bad about any of it later.

Self-care *à la française* is doing what is necessary to find joie de vivre in big and small ways every day.

Opposite

I am very comfortable with my shaved head, red lips, bold earrings, and scarves. I never wait for fancy occassions to wear my most grand dresses.

Above

You don't have to eat
a sugary dessert every
day but when you do,
choose something that
brings you pleasure and
don't feel guilty about it.

REDEFINING THE PLEASURE PRINCIPLE

Plaisir is a word I hear or use every single day in Paris.

When I am at a restaurant, the waiter will ask me, *Ça vous plaît?*—"Does it please you?"

If I invite a friend to come over to my apartment for an *apéro,* they will respond, *avec plaisir*—"with pleasure."

If I run into a friend I haven't seen in a while, she might tell me the next day, *C'était une plaisir de te voir*—"It was a pleasure to see you."

Pleasure is not a luxury, and it is definitely not a dirty word associated only with sex. It's a feeling of happy satisfaction and enjoyment, and that feeling can be derived in many ways. The French are always in pursuit of pleasure, and they abide by an unspoken pleasure principle, which we can all benefit from learning. Basically, if something doesn't please them, they aren't going to do it. And if something *does* bring them pleasure, they sure as heck aren't going to feel guilty for doing it.

The French do not ascribe negative associations to things that make them feel good and satisfied—and we shouldn't, either. In fact, in France, there is no such thing as a "guilty pleasure." Yes, sure, the literal translation of that is *plaisir coupable,* but the phrase is rarely, if ever, used, and definitely not to denigrate desires. (The French do, however, use the term *péché mignon*—literally, a "cute sin," but meaning a "tiny sin.")

The French's motto? Balance and moderation. In other words, don't be so extreme and hard on yourself. You don't need to compartmentalize your pleasure to certain times or moments, because you will likely end up overdoing it and feeling guilty as a result.

My neighbor once invited me over for an *apéro* when I was two days into an intense cleanse. I brought my carrots and a bottle of water to the gathering. When I explained my cleanse, the hostess's expression changed from one of confusion to one of utter horror. I was proudly extolling the benefits of cleanses when she cut me off: "You can have one glass of wine," she said, and then poured me a glass. I accepted the glass *avec plaisir* and savored every sip.

On another occasion, I was having dinner with a friend and her husband. Shortly after announcing that I had given up sweets, I ordered a dessert—which I then inhaled. (It was so good.) I apologized for slopping it up so fast, and my friend's husband said, "Did it bring you pleasure?" I made some groaning sounds to indicate that it had, and he said, "Well, don't be sorry, then."

PLEASURE IS NOT . . .

- supposed to make you feel guilty or inspire regret.

- a luxury or a reward.

- a dirty word used solely for X-rated content.

- torturing yourself with extreme restrictions.

- boring people by blabbering about the latest diet trend.

PLEASURE IS . . .

- allowing yourself to enjoy a sweet treat "just because."

- savoring the present moment and every bite or sip, or vacation day, or manicure, or head massage.

- expressing your feelings of bliss loudly (bonus points for finding the words to express those sounds).

- accepting an invitation to spend time with someone and knowing that their company will bring your soul deep satisfaction.

- consuming culture you enjoy, however trashy, without having to justify or explain it.

The French word *non* means more than just "no." It's a form of self-preservation, protection for one's time and sanity.

JUST SAY NO!

Repeat after me . . .

Non.

Ce n'est pas possible. (It's not possible.)

Ça risque d'être compliqué. (This risks being complicated.)

C'est hors de question. (It's out of the question.)

The French are known for saying *non*. It's an accurate stereotype, and one that is incredibly annoying, driving everyone, especially us *étrangers* (foreigners) crazy. I remember when I lived in France for a summer during graduate school and was craving a ham and cheese sandwich on a baguette with all the fixings. I waltzed into a *boulangerie* in the 20th arrondissement and surveyed the selection of sandwiches: *jambon beurre* (ham and butter), *crudité mayo* (vegetables with mayo), *thon* (tuna) with lettuce and tomato, and a *jambon fromage beurre* (ham, cheese, and butter). I asked if I could order a ham and cheese, but with mayonnaise, lettuce, and tomato.

The woman behind the counter said no.

I said, "Oh yes, sorry. I don't mind paying an additional price."

She still said no.

I thought that, surely, she hadn't understood me correctly. So, I pointed out that she seemed to have a lot of extra cheese and lettuce and a vat of mayo on standby. Why was it not possible? I was growing so frustrated that I wanted to buy the two sandwiches containing my desired ingredients, smash them together in front of her, and storm out of there. At the very least, I planned to huff to anyone who would listen about the *boulangerie*'s poor customer service.

Only recently have I come to understand, and almost appreciate, how easily the French toss out "no" in all its various forms—and why. The French word *non* means more than just "no." It's a form of self-preservation, protection for one's time and sanity. The woman in the *boulangerie* had

Above
Saying no to an invitation
can sometimes mean
more time to sit and
just be.

already prepared those sandwiches and didn't want to personalize or change them up to meet every customer's desire. I had come into her shop, so if I didn't like what she had to offer, I could simply try another bakery.

As an ex–New Yorker, this made no sense to me. I am accustomed to getting what I want when and how I want it. As a result, here in Paris, I have committed some faux pas—asked people on their lunch break to perform a service for me, offered extra money for something to be done faster, and begged friends to come out with me when I knew they weren't feeling up to it. And the answer has always been *non*.

Julie Barlow and Jean-Benoît Nadeau, co-authors of *The Bonjour Effect: The Secret Codes of French Conversation Revealed,* write that, "The French Revolution was about the irrevocable right of all citizens to refuse." The French say no because it's in their blood; it comes from the roots of protest. They say no because they have learned over generations that they have the right to say no. They are a people of protest. This still doesn't quite jell for me, but I have learned to digest it better—and have even adopted the custom for myself, especially when that simple word protects my time, my sanity, and my *bien-être* (well-being).

The next time you're wishy-washy about saying no, remember:

1. Saying no frees up your time to say yes to yourself—or something else.

2. Saying no means not holding yourself back, but rather setting yourself up for inner contentment.

3. When you say yes when you really want to say no, you are doing a disservice both to yourself and to the person whose invitation you are accepting. Nobody wants to be with someone who doesn't really want to be there.

A CHAT WITH
A QUEEN OF
JOIE DE VIVRE

PATRICIA LOUISOR-BROSSET

Life coach, DJ, consultant, fashion designer,
and personal stylist

I met Patricia, a true Parisienne, my first year in
Paris, at a ladies' cocktail gathering that my friend
Tara regularly hosted. A lovely group of women
who have known each other more than twenty
years, they dance, they dine, they travel, and they
lift one another up. Every time I get an invitation
to a party or dinner chez Patricia, I go, because
she embodies joie de vivre, and I immediately feel
her energy rub off on me.

Patricia is one of those friends I wish everyone
had. She is beautiful inside and out. She is
confident. Her smile and laugh are contagious.
She remembers a song or a dish you like and
makes sure to play it or prepare it when you're
with her. She loves to bring pleasure to those
around her, but best of all, she lives life on her
own terms. In thinking about how we can live a
celebratory life full of *joie,* there is no one better
to speak to than Patricia.

Q: What brings you pleasure?

A: I adore cooking and have thirty or forty
cookbooks. It's like meditation or therapy for
me. I love eating as well, but on my own. It's
not always a social thing. For example, I might
go to the market and see beautiful *oursins* (sea
urchins). I'll buy three or four, go home, turn
everything off, shut my eyes, and just enjoy them
tremendously. This is my kind of pleasure. Music,
of course, is another pleasure, and I like to put
on headphones and deeply immerse myself. I
also love going to see contemporary dance, a
good play, or even live art. I *love, love, love, love,
love* that. And I do these things on my own. I
don't have to talk about it. I immerse myself in
something that brings me pleasure, and I keep
it inside.

Q: Do you believe in "guilty pleasures"?

A: *Guilt* is not a word I would ever use. We're all
going to die one day. Are you going to feel guilty
about having another glass of champagne? Of
course not! If it gives you pleasure, please, be my
guest. Have two.

Q: What about saying no?

A: If I don't want to go, I don't want to go.
Especially if I'm not sure. Then no, no, no.
We all have the right to say no without feeling
guilty, because a no to someone [else] is a yes to
yourself.

WHAT WOULD BEYONCÉ DO?

Q: What does *bien-être* mean to you?

A: I love fasting—having one juice in the morning and a soup or a broth in the evening—and I love taking walks. This, for me, is self-care, because I'm working on my longevity. Oh, and I love massages. Your body knows what's good for you. Massages are good for me. Taking long baths is good for me. Stretching is good for me. Pilates and yoga are good for me. I think I'm old enough now to understand what's good for me.

Q: What does the French saying *être bien dans sa peau* ["to be comfortable in one's own skin"] mean to you?

A: Being *bien dans sa peau* is *bien dans son âge* first. "Being happy with your *age*." Why? Because it means that you've *lived*. After that, it's about respecting yourself. If you are able to stop when something doesn't work for you, you are *bien dans sa peau* because you understand who you are and what makes you happy, full, curious, and blessed. You enjoy every second of life. Micro events. This is *bien dans sa peau* for me.

Q: What about joie de vivre? How do you celebrate the good life?

A: It's looking for small things and using your senses. Walking in the market gives me so much joy, because everything is there. The vegetables are alive. The flowers are alive. The fruits are alive. It's so inspiring. All the colors are joie de vivre, too. It's being aware that everything is under your eyes, your nose, and your fingers. Try to use one sense after the other, rather than all at once. This is a more profound experience.

Above
Patricia in her home, where she makes everyone feel welcome and enjoys time alone when she needs it.

Fashions fade, style is eternal.

—Yves Saint Laurent

CULTIVATE CONFIDENCE BY CURATING YOUR STYLE

When I was in high school, I was utterly obsessed with fashion and subscribed to all the magazines I thought mattered: *Vogue, Elle,* and *Harper's Bazaar.* I dreamed of jumping into those editorial pages, wearing couture creations, and lounging on Louis XVI couches in a room surrounded by nineteenth-century moldings and chandeliers. *How lucky Parisiennes must be,* I thought, *to live amongst the kings and queens of fashion*: Yves Saint Laurent, Karl Lagerfeld, and Sonia Rykiel, among others. *They must all wear the latest styles and perfectly piece together looks on a daily basis,* I thought. *People-watching from a corner café must be like sitting in the front row of a fashion show. Their closets must be exploding with designer pieces. Right?*

Wrong. At least, not in the Paris I now inhabit. Now that I live here, I can tell my teenage self that even though Paris is the fashion capital of the world, the place where some of the biggest fashion houses have their headquarters, it is also a place where you can cultivate your own style and gain confidence in it. Why? Because the French are not trend chasers. Parisiennes aren't as obsessed with clothes as you might expect. They don't jump on the next "it" handbag or walk on cobblestone streets in Louboutins. Traditional advertising tactics—"pink is the new black" and "fanny packs are the new bucket bags"—don't really work on the majority of people here. And I love that! Why should my wardrobe be considered old news every few months? Without the pressure of having to replace, replace, replace and update, update, update, you can cultivate a style you like and that works for you for as long as it suits you.

The French do, however, favor and celebrate looking one's best at all times. There's a woman, Madame Da Silva, who is a *gardienne* (a type of superintendent) for several buildings on my street. For the longest time, I have watched her drag trash cans in and out of buildings, sweep entryways, and dash out to drop her grandchildren off at school, and she's always wearing one of her signature looks: either a pantsuit with a silky blouse, a pencil skirt, or a dress. She says she wears the suit only when she rides her bike, but she still sports stacked heels and lipstick. When I asked her why she was always dressed so nicely to clean buildings, she told me that this has always been her "look" and that it gives her confidence. She also shared a French proverb: *Comment tu te presentes, tu sera estimé.* "How you present yourself will be how you are esteemed/regarded/respected/valued/judged."

As for me, I'm American, so there have been days when I've pulled on my Ugg boots to drop my kids off at school in the morning or worn my gym clothes to the market. When I do, though, I always feel judgmental, disapproving eyes looking me up and down. Once, at a café on my street, I ran into a restaurant owner from the hood with whom I'm friendly. He took one look at me and said, "What's going on? You are just giving up?"

At first, I was confused. Then I looked down at my Ugg boots–yoga pants combo. Ouch. The worst, however, was being schooled by my then-six-year-old daughter. It was the height of the pandemic, and we were staying in a little town in the Basque country. After I'd spent a good week in a rotation of sweats and yoga pants, my daughter snuck into my room, laid out a dress for me, added some of my usual bold jewelry, and paired the outfit with pointy-toed flats. She left the ensemble on the bed as a not-so-subtle hint for me to make more of an effort the next time I got dressed. I was flabbergasted. *Who does she think she is?* Well, I guess she's French. And the kid was right. When it comes to style, no matter your mood or the state of the world, self-preservation and self-respect are key. (But I will add this caveat: It's okay to "let loose" and bust out the sweats and yoga pants.)

Above
Strolling through the streets of Dijon in a long, flowy dress cinched at the waist.

CREATE YOUR OWN LOOK

There's no rush to determine what works for you,
but as you embark on the process, remember this:
You don't need to be polished all the time. Focus
on items that bring you joy *and* make you look
good. Only then will it all start to feel effortless.
You won't even have to think about it.

I started collecting scarves because they
remind me of Nigerian women, and wearing
them has become part of my "look." Also, when
I stopped ordering green contact lenses, I began
gravitating toward thick eyeglass frames, to
highlight my natural eye color. It's taken me some
time to settle into my own style, but now I am
happy with it. It feels both natural and unique.
Bold *moi.*

Now when I see ads in the Métro or items
in a shop, I can immediately recognize what will
work for me and what won't. I can also appreciate
pieces that may look fabulous on someone else,
but that would be completely ridiculous on me.
(*Par example,* miniskirts and cropped tops.) Here
are a few tips to help you curate a look that's
uniquely *toi*—"you."

**ACCESSORIES CAN MAKE AN ENTIRE
LOOK.** Something as simple as a black
T-shirt becomes wow-worthy when you
add a beaded statement necklace from
Miriam Haskell. Personally, I love bold
antiques, and modern pieces inspired by
bygone eras. I collect and maybe wear
the same piece for a few weeks before
shopping around (at the *brocantes* or in my
own jewelry box) for others.

**LEARN WHAT SILHOUETTES LOOK
GOOD ON YOU AND STICK WITH
THEM.** You can even create a digital
mood board based on eras, movies, or
people whose style you admire. I'm not
sure what age I was when I realized that I
was totally in love with the 1930s through
the '50s style of cinched waists, A-lines,
and circle skirts, but I now embrace
throwback fashion as if I'm auditioning for
a Hollywood glamour film. I'll add in hints
of the 1980s and '70s, too, in the form of
caftans and long, dramatic, flowy dresses.
These make me feel confident and elegant.

EMBRACE A TRADEMARK PIECE.
When you think about icons, you likely remember the way they personalized their look: Zadie Smith's turban, Diane Keaton's turtleneck, Anna Wintour's bob. Whether it's a specific handbag you break out each winter or a bracelet you wear every day, a signature item not only proves you know yourself, but it makes shopping and dressing easy, too! The same goes for knowing that colors like nude or bright orange do (or don't) work for you. Be confident in your choices, and wear these items with pride. Vintage scarves were the gateway drug to my love of headpieces, including turbans and vintage hats. I usually have a few favorites on regular rotation, but I love adding to my collection and tying them on my head in different ways. This has morphed into my signature style.

CHOOSE A HABITUAL UNIFORM TO SIMPLIFY AND RITUALIZE GETTING DRESSED. While a uniform is a slightly more aggressive form of wearing a signature item, you can be extreme about it à la Karl Lagerfeld; or it can be conceptual. Maybe it's a color you know looks good on you—for me, that's dusty rose—or knowing you don't do pants (like me), and you strictly wear dresses and skirts. I knew that this was my uniform when I showed up to meet my friend Lindsey in pants one day and she expressed a look of shock. (They were 1950s-inspired cigarette pants, *bien sûr,* which is the only exception I make.)

MASTER PLAYING WITH HIGH AND LOW LOOKS FOR FUN, SIMPLICITY, AND BALANCE.
Unwashed hair? Throw on some red lipstick. Leather pants? Pair them with sneakers. I may wear flats, but I won't sacrifice sparkle for comfort, and I'll still throw on a pair of rhinestone earrings with a flowy muumuu. Again, the idea is effortless comfort—but make it chic.

DRESS FOR COMFORT (AND LOOK GREAT, TOO). About ten years ago, I decided my feet needed, *deserved,* to be 100 percent comfortable. Now I live in flats and sneakers. High heels and I had a good run, but this is where I am with footwear, and I'm comfortable with that decision—as are my feet. Still, comfort can't mean being lazy, so I refrain from wearing yoga pants or a jogging suit around town.

Opposite
Vintage and modern scarves have become signature pieces for me. I almost always have one tied around my head or twisted up into a turban.

THE REAL BEAUTY

A fellow expat once used a fascinating analogy to point out how Americans and the French approach presentation differently. In the United States, she said, we usually have two shower curtains: one that actually protects us and one we show to the world. In France, buying one shower curtain—that is both "proper" and practical and that can be maintained for years—is standard. I think we can apply this to beauty, too. Less is, indeed, more. Let's work with what we've got rather than pile on unnecessarily. I once heard the saying *être bien dans sa peau* or *se sentir bien dans sa peau* ("to be good in your skin" or "to feel good in your skin"), and I have worked toward that ever since.

There used to be so many parts of me I hated and wanted to hide or change—parts I now embrace. Big, wide nose? Just like my father's. Big hands and long fingers? Great for layering up all my oversize jewelry. Gapped teeth? The French call them *dents de bonheur,* which means "lucky teeth." Thin, barely-there eyebrows? Just like my mother, whom I miss dearly. These traits make me 100 percent Ajiri. The French are all about embracing your natural self. In fact, there are so many French celebs with distinct traits who are celebrated for their talents despite features that would make them less than perfect by American standards. (See: Vanessa Paradis, Gérard Depardieu, Camille Cottin, and Jean-Pascal Zadi.)

In France, there isn't a perfectionist ideal about beauty, so artifice, enhancements, *changements,* obsessing over everything you want to change, and so on—it isn't really praised. That's not to say that the French don't have surgeries or anything artificial done to them, because they do, but they make sure it's discreet, subtle.

It's this approach that gave me the courage to shave my head. Actually, my daughter had a hand in that. One day, at five years old, she found a pair of scissors and chopped off all her golden curls while I was lying on the couch reading. Then she casually walked past me with a salad bowl full of ringlets on her way to the kitchen, hoping I wouldn't notice or care. I looked up to see only a single curl left on her head and freaked out, but

Beauty begins the moment you decide to be yourself.

—*Coco Chanel*

she unapologetically declared that it was just hair and would grow back. Schooled in the facts by a French five-year-old! Despite being unamused by her actions, I thought it was remarkable how she confidently freed herself of the hair she was sick of dealing with—the same hair I had loved playing with. In fact, I was envious.

A month or so later, I was on a solo vacation in Chantilly days before my thirty-ninth birthday, reflecting in a journal about what I wanted to do differently in my new year. This led me to admit to myself that though I had a lot of goals, and plans for expanding my projects, I felt held back by my constant concern about how my hair looked. I spent so much time and money on it. Like Noomi, I, too, wanted to be free! Free from the maintenance as well as the insecurity I attached to my hair. I went to a store, bought clippers, took my extensions off, and shaved my head right there in that hotel room.

I had been processing or adding extensions to my hair for as long as I could remember, but now I was done. I stared in the mirror at my new look, embracing the moment but still terrified about what people would think of me. I even checked out of

my room the next day wearing a hat. But because I am me, I couldn't resist stopping at a flea market on the way home, and I made myself take the hat off. I walked around an antiques shop actually enjoying the feeling of fresh air on my head.

Back in Paris, everyone embraced me as they normally would have. I returned to my daily life, and when I met up with friends or parents from school, they told me they loved my new hairstyle. My husband told me I looked beautiful, and my daughter was, of course, proud of having inspired my chop. It sounds a bit silly to admit that I ever thought otherwise, but nobody liked me any more or less because of my sudden lack of hair.

Maybe I will grow my hair back out one day, maybe I will get extensions or braids again, and maybe I won't. But who cares? I went from spending lots of money on extensions and hair treatments at the salon to heading to a barbershop for a ten-euro shave every few weeks.

You know what else I've stopped buying so much of? Makeup. I just don't wear it every day. Most days, I just use a little mascara and slap on some red lipstick—that's it.

Between my hair and my face, I am no longer shelling out money, wasting time, or feeling stress and insecurity. Now that I have learned how good it feels to be myself, I am no longer looking to transform myself into someone I saw in a magazine or online.

THE ABCs OF FRENCH BEAUTY

Opposite

I like to keep my makeup bag simple with red lipstick from Fenty and Guerlain, and mascara from YSL.

- **UNLESS YOU'LL BE ATTENDING A PARTY IN YOUR DREAMS, NEVER GO TO BED WEARING MAKEUP.** Always remove it before shut-eye time. And even if you don't wear any, you still need to clean your face from the day.

- **BEAUTY REALLY IS SKIN DEEP.** You can cover it up all you want, but under the layers is the real you—and that "you" deserves care and attention.

- **AGING IS INEVITABLE.** Until someone finds the fountain of youth, don't fight it. Rather, slow it down with a daily routine, natural skin products, and monthly treatments.

- **DON'T IGNORE YOUR NECK.** It might be part of your face one day.

- **BE DISCREET.** If you decide to do a treatment like Botox, keep that information to yourself. No one needs to know how or why you suddenly lost your laugh lines. Isn't the whole point to look natural?

- **REMEMBER THIS THREE-WORD BEAUTY MANTRA:** Prevention, care, and maintenance. Looking after your skin from head to toe on a regular basis is the most important way to prevent damage.

- **SAVE YOUR CENTIMES.** Taking care of your skin doesn't need to break the bank. In fact, the French go to the pharmacy for most of their beauty care and are often skeptical of expensive products (see "French Beauty Essentials," page 256).

- **KEEP IT LIGHT.** Unless you're performing onstage, a full face of makeup isn't always necessary. There is no need to clog your pores by slathering on too much foundation. A quick application of mascara and a glide of some lipstick will go a long way.

- **SPRITZ IT, DON'T SPRAY IT.** No one wants to be the person whose scent is so strong that strangers on a crowded Métro come away smelling like it. A light spritz behind each ear and on both wrists is more than enough. Moderation is key.

- **EFFORTLESS BEAUTY TAKES EFFORT.** It may sound like an oxymoron, but believe me: No one "just woke up like this." If everyone can tell, then it's too much.

- **TREAT YOURSELF TO TREATMENTS.** Parisians regularly visit their aesthetician or *institut de beauté* for facials, scrubs, and massages. Such treatments are calming, yes, but also a part of maintenance and self-care.

FRENCH BEAUTY ESSENTIALS

The French *loooove* their beauty products, most of which they buy at the pharmacy when refilling their prescriptions. But they also *loooove* to take care of the skin they were born in, and maintenance requires many different gels, creams, spritzes, sprays, and serums. Morning and evening rituals have become rather calming moments for me—I feel like I am honoring my body and doing something proactive by taking care of it. It's as if, with each wipe and caress, I am celebrating my face.

Here's a list of what you'll find in my (and many of my friends') medicine cabinet and some brands I enjoy. (Most are French, but a few others have slipped in over time.)

- **MICELLAR WATER:** Avène Eau Micellaire
- **SERUM:** La Roche-Posay Sérum à la Vitamine C
- **EYE CREAM:** Darphin Eye Care Sérum
- **THERMAL WATER SPRAY:** Avène Eau Thermale
- **TOOLS:** Round cotton pads, paper tissues, a jade roller
- **SCRUBS AND FACE MASKS:** Filorga Sheet Hydra-Filler Mask; Klorane Eye Patches
- **TONER:** Caudalie Beauty Elixir Toner
- **NIGHTTIME MOISTURIZER:** Darphin Hydraskin Rich Crème; Embryolisse Lait-Crème Concentré
- **DAYTIME MOISTURIZER:** Guerlain Abeille Royale Crème Jour; Avène Hydrance Aqua-Gel
- **ADDITIONAL CARE:** Dr. Hauschka Clarifying Steam Bath (for face)
- **SKIN REPAIR CREAM:** Avène Cicalfate Restorative Skin Cream
- **BODY OILS:** Nuxe Huile Prodigieuse; Officine Universelle Buly Huile
- **BODY LOTION:** Topicrem Ultra-Hydratant Lait Corps (body milk); Avène Baume Fondant Hydratant
- **SPF:** La Roche-Posay Anthelios Brume Fraîche Invisible 50+
- **PERFUME:** Rituals Maharaja; Chanel Allure; Guerlain Shalimar; Frédéric Malle Portrait of a Lady

A CASE FOR THERMAL SPAS

We can thank the Greeks and Romans for discovering the benefits of natural freshwater hot springs and seawater therapy. Apparently, they'd get so worn out from battle that they'd soak their wounds and fatigued muscles in water to heal, rejuvenate, and relax. In fact, the treatments they'd partake in were called *sanitas per aquam* in Latin, hence the word *spa*. Of course, the Greeks and Romans weren't the only ones getting in on the aqua action: Egyptians and Israelites used to plunge themselves in the Nile and Jordan rivers, while Hindus headed toward the Ganges to heal their aching bodies and souls.

Somewhere along the way, the French realized that there was something to healing oneself with water and built towns around mineral springs—and France became the unofficial European capital of thermal spas.

In order to be designated a true thermal spa, the property must adhere to a certain number of criteria, such as having been called such dating back to the nineteenth century or earlier; having an active water source used for bathing or drinking as part of the center; and possessing thermal architecture dating back to at least the nineteenth century, including balneotherapy-related buildings classified as historic monuments (essentially, ones with baths used solely for soaking, not exercise or movement). Also, to be considered a true *thalassothérapie* spa—meaning, only seawater is used—a spa must be located near the original water source. This is why many thalassotherapy spas tend to be on or near the coast, of which France has much of.

But short of tossing some sea salt into a bath or positioning oneself in front of Jacuzzi jets, what's the real draw here? Once again, it's another opportunity to find *joie* by slowing down and taking care of oneself. In fact, with a prescription from a doctor, the French can spend three weeks at a thermal spa and it will be covered under their health plan—including food and transportation. Kinda shocking, right? But since thermal water itself is sourced from natural springs, wells, or the sea, it contains a variety of minerals, such as selenium and magnesium, that are extremely beneficial for hydrating skin, reversing UV damage, and balancing the microbiome. Other reasons for visiting a thermal or thalassotherapy spa include circulation problems, arthritis, depression, and weight issues. Treatments, called *cures,* run the gamut from the relaxing and basic (say, soaking in a whirlpool) to the active and bold (say, the *longe–côte marche aquatique,* where you walk sideways into the ocean, against the current, to increase circulation and burn fat by way of resistance to the cold, nutrient–filled seawater. A friend did this and said it was remarkably invigorating!).

It's only a matter of time before I head to my general practitioner and ask for a prescription. Writing a book, being a mom, *and* running a business is hard work. I'll bet my doc would write me a script just for being an American who constantly needs a "cure" to remind herself to slow down and enjoy life.

A SPA HIT LIST

Whether you're in it for the feeling or the
healing, France has an extraordinary number of
spas (thermal or otherwise) worthy of your time
and, *oui,* your money. Is there really a price on, as
Nina Simone sings, feeling good? Here are a few
of my picks for general and thermal spas both in
Paris and the rest of France.

IN PARIS

SPA GUERLAIN. I love history and design just
as much as I love beauty treatments. (One
is for the brain, the other for the body, but
both for joy.) The Guerlain spas housed
in the Saint James Paris and the Relais
Christine, sister hotels and nineteenth-
century mansions, check off all the boxes.
The spa in the Relais Christine is set under
the thirteenth-century vaults of a former
abbey. The Saint James Paris was built in
honor of former French president Adolphe
Thiers by his widow, and it later became
a dormitory for students. I have tried the
two-hour La Dédicace on a day that I
dedicated to much needed solo time, and
also tried the face sculpt on an occasion for
necessary skin maintenance.

MOLITOR SPA, BY CLARINS. Make a
day of it and head out to Paris's art deco
swimming pool and club Molitor (where
the bikini debuted in 1946) to relax at the
largest spa and fitness center in Europe.
At seventeen thousand square feet, with
thirteen cabins and a private suite with a
sauna, hammams (steam rooms), lounge
beds, and more, the Molitor offers a
vacation in the center of the city.

O'KARI HAMMAM/SPA. If you're looking
for something more DIY, or want to go
with a group of girlfriends but don't want
to break the bank, this female-only, multi-
bath hammam near rue Montorgueil is
amazing. There are no frills, but the place
is clean and atmospheric (like being in
Morocco), and you will leave feeling
rejuvenated—especially if you opt for a
black soap scrub and an almond hair wash.

OUTSIDE OF PARIS

SPA ET BISTROT LOISEAU DES SENS, BURGUNDY. This one's especially great for foodies, because it's part of the famed Michelin-starred Le Relais Bernard Loiseau, in pinot noir territory. After you've stuffed yourself silly at the restaurant, take your food coma over to the self-dubbed "multi-sensory pleasure universe," which includes various pools (some with massage alcoves), a Hydronox sofa, saunas, showers (hot and cold), and more.

ÉVIAN RESORT, ÉVIAN-LES-BAINS. Evian is quite possibly the most famous bottled water in the world, but maybe you've never really thought about where it comes from or why it's so good for you. (Don't worry, I hadn't, either.) On the sparkling shores of Lake Geneva in the French Alps is the mothership of natural spa towns. "Official" Évian cures and treatments can be booked at two storied and popular hotels: the Hôtel Royal and the Hôtel Ermitage. But all properties in the region use local water, so no matter where you decide to stay, sip, or bathe, you'll be benefiting from some of the finest water out there—water that is naturally enhanced with minerals and electrolytes thanks to a spring source located at the base of peaks and glaciers in France's Auvergne-Rhône-Alpes region.

VILLA LA COSTE, PROVENCE. There's nothing water-focused about this landlocked property surrounded by vineyards in the middle of Provence. But if you need an excuse to wander in the more private part of the otherwise open-to-the-public château, with its monumental contemporary art installations, I suggest booking a treatment at Villa La Coste. It'll be another splurge—one that begins with a sniff test to choose your oil scent—but it'll be worth it. Trust me.

CURES MARINES, TROUVILLEHÔTEL, THALASSO SEA AND SPA, TROUVILLE, NORMANDY. Located in the *très* charming town of Trouville, this spa is home to the aforementioned *longe-côte* ocean treatment my friend enjoyed, wetsuit and all. Other seawater-based remedies include cryotherapy tubs, algae wraps, and multiday programs that include a little of everything for anyone staying in the 103-room hotel facing the sea.

Following page
Spa Guerlain at the Saint James Paris.

MORE SOURCES OF *JOIE*

All addresses listed are for Paris, unless otherwise noted.

BOOKSTORES

- **Artazart:** 83 Quai de Valmy, 75010
- **Librairie Galignani:** 224 rue de Rivoli, 75001
- **Shakespeare and Company:** 37 rue de la Bûcherie, 75005
- **Smith & Son Paris:** 248 rue de Rivoli, 75001

CAFÉS

- **Bistro Saint Dominique:** 131 rue Saint-Dominique, 75007
- **Les Sans Culottes:** 27 rue de Lappe, 75011
- **Salon de thé Rose Bakery in the Musée de la Vie Romantique:** 16 rue Chaptal, 75009
- **La Perle:** 78 rue Vieille-du-Temple, 75003
- **Le Progrès:** 7 rue des Trois Frères, 75018
- **Le Roussillon:** 186 rue de Grenelle, 75007
- **Le Saint-Régis:** 6 rue Jean du Bellay, 75004
- **L'Eclair:** 32 rue Cler, 75007
- **Le Grand Salon:** Hôtel Particulier Montmartre, 23 avenue Junot Pavillon D, 75018
- **Le Hibou:** 16 Carr de l'Odéon, 75006
- **Fabula in the Musée Carnavalet:** 16 rue des Francs-Bourgeois, 75004
- **Malabar:** 88 rue Saint-Dominique, 75007
- **Treize au Jardin:** 5 rue de Médicis, 75006

OUT-OF-TOWN CHÂTEAUX

- **Château de Brécy:** 8 Route du Château, 14480 Creully sur Seulles
- **Château de Marqueyssac:** Les Jardins de Marqueyssac, 24220 Vézac
- **Château du Champ de Bataille:** 8 Route du Chateau, 27110 Sainte-Opportune-du-Bosc
- **Château La Ballue:** La Ballue, 35560 Bazouges-la-Pérouse
- **Manoir d'Eyrignac:** Les Jardins du Manoir d'Eyrignac, 24590 Salignac-Eyvigues
- **Saint-André Abbey:** rue Montée du Fort, 30400 Villeneuve-lès-Avignon

PARKS AND GARDENS

- **Jardin Albert Khan:** 2 rue du Port, 92100 Boulogne-Billancourt
- **Parc Monceau:** 35 boulevard de Courcelles, 75008
- **Square Gardette:** 24 rue Saint-Ambroise, 75011

STREETS AND AREAS

- The *bouquinistes* (booksellers) along the Seine
- Coulée verte René Dumont
- Galerie Vivienne
- Passage des Panoramas
- Passage Verdeau
- Rue de Mouzaïa
- Rue des Martyrs
- Rue du Bac
- Rue Montorgueil

ACKNOWLEDGMENTS

Creating this book while running a business and raising two young children has been one of the most challenging experiences that was, nonetheless, full of joy thanks to so many gracious and generous people. This book only exists because of the people—my tribe—who supported me throughout the entire process. They say it takes a village to raise a child, but it also takes one to develop and write a book. (This list also resembles my dinner party guest list, which is usually pretty long too!)

First of all, if it wasn't for my super agent, Leigh Eisenman, this book would still only exist in café conversations. Thank you to Madame Leigh for more-than-simple support but for much-needed guidance and endless encouragement. Should our next rendezvous be at Joe T's in Fort Worth or Le Nemours in Paris?

I am extremely grateful to my editor, Angelin Adams, for her confidence in me and for giving me this opportunity and a platform to share my stories with the world. Thank you for allowing me to share openly and for always listening and supporting me.

To Jessica Antola, the photographer behind most of the beautiful photographs in this book, thank you for sharing these moments with me. It has been a full-circle experience to work on this with you after meeting over ten years ago at a party in New York City and talking all evening about our shared love of Paris.

To Sara Lieberman and Krystal Kenney, thank you for your individual talents and invaluable support in helping me cross the finish line. I couldn't have gotten here without you both.

Merci to Guillaume Sardin for your delightful illustrations that added Parisian charm to the pages of this book.

Thank you to my St. Jo saviors who graciously shared stories, endured all my cultural faux pas, and took my kids for sleepovers, vacations, and playdates so that I could write: Astrid Martin, David Martin, Laura Nové-Josserand, David Bossan, Sonja Tanaka, Maxime Leboussou, Priscilla Bertin, Raphäel Dautigny, Nelly Vaz, and Remi Galipienso.

Expat life is made so much sweeter when friends become family and I am lucky to have so many. Thank you to my "Dream Girls" who provided comic relief and attended brainstorming gatherings when stress and deadlines loomed. To Vanessa Grall, thank you for reading early pages, sharing your knowledge of the lesser-known gems of Paris, constant creative consultation, and opening your beautiful home for photoshoots and gatherings. (The Mill is officially a cover beauty!) To Sonja Tanaka, thank you for being my writing retreat companion, helping me work through concepts, and helping me as a creative producer and photo shoot assistant. My expat life turned to feeling like my home life thanks to you. To Kristin Frederick, thank you for helping with French food matters. And to Emma Gilkeson, thank you for always showing up to lend a hand behind the scenes (and sometimes lending your face for photo shoots).

To my AC ladies, Lauren Collins and Lindsey Tramuta, thank you for providing me with a bottomless well of thought-provoking articles, dinner discussions, feedback, and advice. Having each written books of your own, you both have always been so generous in sharing wisdom and experiences, and I am grateful for all of it. There is no one I would rather take up space at cafés around Paris with.

There have been so many friends in Paris who have been my cheerleaders and dinner guests for fellowship and hashing out ideas around (usually beautifully set) tables. Thank you to Monique Benoit for supporting me in moments during our family sabbatical to work and for reminders to be thankful for moments of joy. To Zeva Bellel, merci for countless café dates, phone calls, pandemic brainstorm dates, and helping me to see *joie* as the North Star. You are an amazing listener and connector of the dots. To Cassi Bryn Michalik and Emilie Minandier, thank you for all the impromptu *apéros,* and especially to Emilie for opening your home for last-minute marathon photo shoots. To Mary Gallagher, Tanis Kmetyk, and India Kmetyk, thank you for sharing your Paris lessons with me. To Sonya Hofer and Benjamin Lanz, thank you for picnics on the Seine and across the parks of Paris. To Nesrine and Jonas, merci for your support and offering the French version of southern hospitality.

To my dear David Lipke and Marie-Noel Bauer, thank you for dropping everything to read early versions of the manuscript. Your encouragement and confirmation were a much-needed push.

A big merci to friends across oceans who still found ways to gather and support me despite the distance: Tara Ballarotto for being a mentor and connector; Julie Tran Lê and Kim West for being my biggest supporters and cheerleaders in life since my days of unsuccessfully searching for joy in NYC; George Sotelo and Michelle Stein, who always make time to break bread with me; and Genny Cortinovis and Tom Schmidt for giving me and my family a beautiful Provençal backdrop to sort through book edits.

To all my Torbes, gracias for lively group chats, steady encouragement, and all those epic *jeuvesitos* that I miss so badly. Thursdays will always feel like a good day to gather because of you. And an extra gracias to Eugenia Gonzalez, Ximena Gonzalez, Amanda Alvarez, and Paloma Alvarez, for teaching me fellowship the Mexican way and sharing Teresa, Marcela, and Paloma—your aunties and mothers—with me.

I deeply appreciate everyone who took time to talk to me for the book and allowed me to profile them or serve as a source of information on French culture. Thank you to David Martin and David Bossan for schooling me on what a real baguette is. To Matthieu Magnaudeix and Lucas Armati, thank you for late night conversations about French culture and power. To Amy LaKupec Larue, I appreciate you taking me back to my landscape design class and making time to chat on drives to the gardens in Chartres and Blois. To Bertrand Fairerol, Caroline Grangie, and Raphäel Dautigny, thank you for sharing your childhood mealtime memories with me. Thank you to Sharri Harmel from *Extra Ordinary Women* for sharing Amy with me. To Audrey Neracoulis, Ciara, and COIFFURE, merci for sharing beauty secrets that I could try and steal. Lucas Somoza and Thierry Wasser, thank you for my first welcome dinner in Paris and talking to me about beauty. I am grateful to Guillaume Féau of Féau Boiseries for taking the time to share his treasure trove. Merci to Nicolas Egloff and his team at the Hotel Saint James and Relais Christine for welcoming me. And thank you to the beauty team at Guerlain.

A big merci to my friends who shared their thoughts on joie de vivre for "chats" in this book: Frank Barron, Vanessa Grall, Mireille d'Ardhuy-

Santiard, Tanisha Townsend, Laura Adrian, Braden Perkins, Amy Kupec Larue, Aline Asmar d'Amman, and Patricia Louisor-Brosset.

I am very grateful to the women at Madame de la Maison who helped keep the business moving while I worked on this book and also assisted me with research, transcribing, and photo shoots. Merci to Hannah Arrasmith, Grace Rempala, Madeline Bobo, and Terri Morris.

The definitions of and differentiation between joy and happiness in Brené Brown's *Atlas of the Heart* helped me dive deeper into understanding the two, and why the French can complain a lot yet still possess so much *joie*. Thank you Brené for inspiring me from afar.

I wrote part of the draft of this book at café in Paris called Le Voyageur. I was inspired by the crew who strolled in daily to read newspapers, sipped solo on the terrace, discussed where they bought the best wine, cheese, or olives, and laughed or argued over current events. This community of people, whom I didn't even know, fueled and strengthened my love of café life and the spirit of joy that people find when sitting with no agenda at a café. Sadly, that café closed shortly after I turned in my manuscript and I don't know the names of the many characters I regularly encountered, except the first names of the previous owner Jasmine and the bartender Jallil. Merci to Le Voyageur (which means "the traveler") and your passengers who helped me escape to work on this book. It was a fleeting moment but one that will stay with me for life.

Joie is not only my book, but it also belongs to the incredible team at Clarkson Potter that worked long and hard with understanding, passion, and enthusiasm to bring it to life. To Robert Diaz, thank you for taking a pile of words and visuals to design this beautiful book. To Sohayla Farman, production editor, merci for making sure all the words make sense and for the encouragement to push me through the final stages. To Heather Williamson, associate director of production, thank you for proofing the massive volume of images for this book. To Lauren Chung, publicist, and Joey Lozada, marketer, merci for your enthusiasm and support in sharing this book and its message.

I must acknowledge the members of my support system who have passed on: my grandmother Hazel, as well as my mother, Cynthia, and her sisters, Auntie Louise and Auntie Ida. It is absolutely because of these women, who modeled joy for me and my brothers, that I love opening my doors, sitting around tables and couches talking too loud, singing badly without shame, spontaneously bursting into dance, telling and retelling the same stories (often exaggerated with imitations), cackling, and never knowing when to call it a night. Mom, you may have not liked using your good china but you sure knew how to live a life full of *joie*.

Thank you to my amazing family: my big brother, Collins Aki, who I still look up to with starry eyes; my forever little big brother, Chester Aki, who is pure love and encouragement; and my sisters-in-love, Yvette Aki and Jenny Yoder. Thank you for the hard truths and unconditional support throughout this project.

A grand merci to Thomas, my husband, for his love and support. We missed getting to have you be a part of many of the behind the scenes of this book project but are so proud of the projects you were working on when you were away.

Finally, thank you to my darlings Noomi and Baz. Sitting at tables with you and finding joy in life every day is messy, hilarious, and beautiful . . . just as it should be.

INDEX

Published in the United States by Clarkson
Potter/Publishers, an imprint of Random
House, a division of Penguin Random
House LLC, New York.
ClarksonPotter.com
RandomHouseBooks.com

CLARKSON POTTER is a trademark and
POTTER with colophon is a registered
trademark of Penguin Random House LLC.

Cataloging-in-Publication Data is on file
with the Library of Congress.
Library of Congress Control Number:
2022028324

ISBN 978-0-593-23657-4
eISBN 978-0-593-23658-1

Printed in China

Photographer: Jessica Antola
Editor: Angelin Borsics
Editorial Assistant: Darian Keels
Designer: Robert Diaz
Production Editor: Sohayla Farman
Production Manager: Heather Williamson
Compositors: Merri Ann Morrell and
Hannah Hunt
Copy Editor: Jenna Dolan
Proofreader: Chris Jerome
Indexer: Amy Hall
Marketer: Joseph Lozada
Publicist: Lauren Chung

Book and cover design by: Robert Diaz
Cover photographs by: Jessica Antola

10 9 8 7 6 5 4 3 2 1

First Edition